# LINGUISTIC STEREOTYPING
# AND MINORITY GROUPS
# IN JAPAN

The public use of language deemed by certain groups within a society to be demeaning to their members has been widely debated in Japan, as in other countries. Such language is known in Japanese as *sabetsu yōgo* (discriminatory language). Japan has no laws attempting to regulate the use of this language; nevertheless, debate on the use of *sabetsu yōgo* has brought about some degree of awareness and modification of language use in differing arenas. These changes have not gone unquestioned; the issue of minority rights versus freedom of speech has been a subject of considerable debate in Japan and elsewhere.

This book is the first full-length study in English of this aspect of language in Japan. Focusing on an aspect of language and power which illustrates some of the dissent underlying Japan's officially promoted ideology of a harmonious society, it discusses the use of linguistic stereotyping in the areas of status, ethnicity, gender and disability, and examines the strategies which have been employed against it.

**Nanette Gottlieb** is Reader in Japanese and Head of the School of Languages and Comparative Cultural Studies, University of Queensland.

# ROUTLEDGE CONTEMPORARY JAPAN SERIES

# LINGUISTIC STEREOTYPING AND MINORITY GROUPS IN JAPAN

*Nanette Gottlieb*

**Routledge**
Taylor & Francis Group

LONDON AND NEW YORK

First published 2006
by Routledge
2 Park Square, Milton Park,
Abingdon, Oxon, OX14 4RN

Simultaneously published in the USA and Canada
by Routledge
270 Madison Ave, New York NY10016

*Routledge is an imprint of the Taylor & Francis Group*

Transferred to Digital Printing 2010

© 2006 Nanette Gottlieb

Typeset in Times New Roman by Graphicraft Limited, Hong Kong

*British Library Cataloguing in Publication Data*
A catalogue record for this book is available from the British Library

*Library of Congress Cataloging in Publication Data*
A catalog record for this book has been requested

ISBN10: 0-415-33803-4 (hbk)
ISBN10: 0-415-59933-4 (pbk)

ISBN13: 978-0-415-33803-5 (hbk)
ISBN13: 978-0-415-59933-7 (pbk)

# CONTENTS

# ACKNOWLEDGEMENTS

Sincere thanks are due to the many people who have helped me with the research for this book. The Australian Research Council and the University of Queensland provided the funding which enabled the research. My two wonderful research assistants, Dr Akemi Dobson and Dr Gayathri Haththotuwa Gamage, outdid themselves in their attention to detail, helpful suggestions and liaison with a wide range of people. Japanese interviewees were generous with time, introductions and information. I would like to thank the staff of the Nissan Institute of Japanese Studies at St Antony's College, Oxford, who extended me their hospitality as a Senior Associate Member during Michaelmas term in 2002. I am deeply indebted to colleagues at the University of Queensland and at universities in the United Kingdom, the United States and Japan who have commented on drafts or seminar presentations of the research and made useful suggestions.

Parts of this book have appeared (in somewhat different form) in the *Asian Studies Review* (1998) and in *Disability & Society* (2001). They have been supplemented with a great deal of original research undertaken since the time of their original publication.

And finally, I could never have finished the book without the untiring love and support of my husband, Hans, and our children, Susan and Greg. I thank them for making it possible.

# INTRODUCTION

For many years now, minority groups in Japan have taken issue with the use of derogatory language and stereotyping referring to their members in the media and other arenas of public discourse. By playing on the fear of public embarrassment on the part of print and visual media organizations through complaints coupled with threats – and in many cases, use – of public denunciation, they have been successful in having certain language banned from use. While such language protests and even public pickets have on occasion also been seen in other countries, they have been particularly effective in the Japanese context because of Japan's 'shame' culture in which the desire to avoid public embarrassment and loss of face is very strong.

One particular activist group, the Buraku Liberation League (BLL), has been the driving force in this process and has spoken up on behalf of other groups from time to time. The Burakumin are Japan's largest minority group, with estimates of their numbers varying from 1.2 million in different encyclopedias to 3 million. Although they are Japanese, physically indistinguishable from their compatriots, they are subject to severe social discrimination, many being descendants of what were in the pre-modern period hereditary outcasts whose occupations had to do with polluting activities. During the Tokugawa Period (1603–1867, also known as the Edo Period), they were forced to live in segregated hamlets ('Buraku' – the term 'burakumin' means 'people of the hamlet') outside the mainstream communities, and were subject to strict rules of conduct. Although the former outcasts were in principle liberated from their lowly status by the Emancipation Edict of 1871, discrimination continued unabated and in the early twentieth century a national organization, the forerunner of today's BLL, was formed to combat it. One of the defining principles of the group's activities was that derogatory language in any form of media or public place would be confronted and overturned, using a tactic known as 'kyūdan' (denunciation) involving public confrontations. It is as a result of this policy that the mass media have developed since the 1970s lists of words to be avoided lest they occasion the embarrassment of a public protest. Other activist organizations of people with disabilities, resident ethnic communities and the indigenous Ainu minority have followed the example of the BLL so that terms referring to their members were also added to the list of terms to be either avoided altogether ('kinkushū') or replaced with a sanitized alternative ('iikaeshū'). On the surface this appears to be a desirable result. The undesirable side-effect, however, in the case of the BLL, has been a muzzling of public discussion rather than an open and neutrally framed discussion of BLL human rights issues, as the media became their own best police.

This book examines the terms, the debate and the processes through which the arguments over linguistic stereotyping have been played out and also touches on the growing phenomenon of hate speech on the internet. The groups I have included in this study are those which have experienced the most compelling examples of linguistic stereotyping on the grounds of status (the Burakumin), ethnicity (Japan's indigenous Ainu minority, resident ethnic communities and foreigners), disability (people with physical and mental disabilities) and gender (women). Each of these groups has succeeded, some to a greater extent than others, in having the terms they find contentious changed in the media, although women still have some way to go. This list is by no means exhaustive, of course: members of Japan's gay communities, atomic bomb victims, Okinawans and many other groups have had similar experiences with language.

The boundaries of these sections of the community are permeable; there are Ainu people with disabilities, for example, and Burakumin women and Koreans living in Burakumin areas. Nor are the groups singled out homogeneous in their internal make-up: as great a diversity exists within each group as exists (though largely unacknowledged) in the community at large. When it comes to language describing them by their defining characteristic, however, be it ethnicity or gender or something else, they are lumped together as a homogeneous whole for the purpose of easy us-and-them categorization, and it is by and large in recognition of this that they have protested such stereotyping. This research engages with the question of the effectiveness of that process of protest in dealing with the discourse of public life in Japan in terms of how that discourse refers to them.

Rather than a top-down policy approach, it is grassroots interest groups that have brought about the changes in public language.

Community protest has been very much a coordinated struggle driven largely by the BLL, who later also lent their support to Ainu people, ethnic Koreans, women and people with disabilities. It is difficult to argue that any underlying concern for socially inclusive language led to the development of the editorial lists that resulted from the language protests. They evolved rather as a kneejerk reaction to fear of adverse publicity and a desire not to be seen to offend rather than from any self-motivated campaign to effect a change in public attitudes, and have been criticized on this account as no more than a face-saving measure which does nothing to address underlying systemic discrimination. Nevertheless, they focus public attention on the issue of what kind of language ought properly to be used to refer to minorities in public discourse, so that the fact of their existence keeps the issue alive.

As in other countries, editorial restrictions inevitably brought a backlash on the grounds that they were no more than political correctness in action and that they militated against the freedom of speech enshrined in the Constitution. It is concern for the protection of this constitutional right which has led Japan to resist United Nations pressure to enact a racial discrimination law, as stipulated in the *United Nations Convention on the Elimination of Racial Discrimination*, to which Japan is a signatory. The argument, as always, comes down to freedom of speech as against human rights and the freedom to live without overt vilification.

Acknowledgement of the discriminatory aspects of particular language – or at least, avoidance of such language – has become second nature to the mass media in 2004. Dictionary publishers have begun to indicate either through tags or through long explanations that particular words are indicators of discrimination. An example: a press release in June 2004 advertising a three-in-one edition of the *Kōjien* (Japan's most prestigious monolingual dictionary), the *Gendai Yōgo no Kiso Chishiki* (*Basic Knowledge of Current Terms*) and a *Ruigo Jiten* (*Dictionary of Synonyms*) mentioned that as certain words were tagged as 'sabetsugo' (discriminatory language), users would be able to check up on 'correct usage'. No such tags were to be found in dictionaries 30 years ago.

The following chapters discuss the parameters of the debate and then the manner in which it has played out in four particular areas: status discrimination, ethnicity, disability and gender. To conclude with just a couple of small editorial notes: Japanese names are given surname first. No page numbers are given for references cited from online sources.

# 1
# LANGUAGE AND REPRESENTATION
## The guidelines

What constitutes discriminatory language, or indeed whether language can even be said to be discriminatory or not, was widely debated in the late twentieth century and remains far from settled today. Each year the media report continuing skirmishes over language, as the following examples show:

- In the United States in 2001, the Cartoon Network, which had planned a Bugs Bunny festival showing every Bugs cartoon made since 1938, withdrew certain of the series made in the 1940s which depicted Bugs 'being offensive to blacks, Indians, Eskimos, Germans and Japanese'. The original plan had been to show the cartoons late at night with the disclaimer: 'These vintage cartoons are presented as representative of the time in which they were created and are presented for their historical value'. Fearing a backlash, however, the network executives banned their showing altogether (*Courier Mail* 2001a).
- In the United Kingdom a few months later, the British Advertising Standards Authority dismissed a complaint against the use of the word 'kraut' – used as a term of abuse meaning 'German' since World War I – in an advertisement, on the grounds that the word is 'a light-hearted reference to a national stereotype unlikely to cause serious or widespread offence'. The German Embassy disagreed (*Courier Mail* 2001b).
- In Melbourne, a large advertising billboard greeted travellers leaving the main airport with an invitation: 'Sexist. Insulting. Demeaning. Vote for your favourite billboard'. That same month a top-rating Australian TV medical drama had a nurse describe a patient as 'mentally challenged'.
- In Japan, academics caused a fuss by proposing to rename birds, animals and fish because elements of their popular names,

1

specifically the words 'dwarf', 'blind' and 'stupid', were deemed discriminatory. The scientific names of the creatures were to remain unchanged. 'Mekura kamemushi' (blind bugs, the popular name for insects of the *Miridae* genus) and 'mekura unagi' (blind eels) have both had their names changed to avoid the use of the contested word 'mekura'. Penguins once referred to as 'kobito' (dwarf penguin) are now called by the English name 'fairy penguin' to avoid reference to dwarfs. A national survey found that 37 of 354 wildlife facilities across Japan have removed a creature from display because its name might offend sensibilities (*Mainichi Shimbun* 2001a).

More recently, in November 2004, the New South Wales Administrative Decisions Tribunal deemed two well-known broadcasters and their Sydney radio station guilty under the Anti-Discrimination Act of homosexual vilification in on-air comments about two gay contestants in reality TV show *The Block* (Sexton and Leys 2004).

Clearly, interest in linguistic stereotyping remains keen. But the interest does not always relate only to tightening controls on language: in October 2004 the West Australian government passed an amendment to proposed racial vilification laws in that state, permitting the terms 'pom' (British migrant), 'wog' (person of Semitic or Mediterranean background) and 'ding' (person of Italian descent) to be used without fear of prosecution because they are 'light-hearted' references to another person's race (Mayes 2004). In other Australian states such as New South Wales and Victoria, the use of these words can lead to civil proceedings. It is unclear whether any 'wogs', 'dings' or 'poms' were consulted in arriving at this decision.

Language and power in any given society, as has long been recognized, are closely linked. 'Disputes about the proper names for people and things are ultimately power struggles. Who has the right to decide how a person shall be called decides how that person shall be classified and defined' (Romaine 1999: 298). The most immediately visible examples of the power plays implicated in language use – leaving aside the wider issues of minority languages within a society and concentrating on language use within the major language – are sexist and racist language, along with other kinds of language which stigmatizes or excludes certain sections of the community.

Many books have been written in Japan on derogatory language, both academic and non-academic, ranging from descriptive collections of incidents where offensive language has been used and challenged (Takagi 1999) to sociological dissections (Yagi 1994).

Most of them have appeared from the mid-1980s to the present, with the majority being published in the early 1990s (although some were much earlier). Yagi (1994: 1–2) speaks of three waves of debate over discriminatory language occurring roughly ten years apart, in the mid-1970s, mid-1980s and mid-1990s. Whereas the first two were driven by activist groups or those closely involved with them, the third centred around writers; the first two took place in relatively closed contexts, but the third made headlines in the press, on TV and in popular magazines. We shall see as this book proceeds how each stage unfolded, and will add a fourth stage of our own.

The terminology of the debate includes 'sabetsu yōgo' (discriminatory language), 'sabetsugo' (discriminatory language) and 'sabetsu hyōgen' (linguistic stereotyping, not necessarily involving any use of contested terms but presenting a particular group of people in an unfavourable light). None of these now common terms is defined in either the 1955 or 1976 editions of Japan's premier monolingual dictionary, the *Kōjien*. They came to prominence with the rise of minority group language protests of various kinds in the 1970s and 1980s. The BLL, who will be discussed in detail in Chapter 3, had been active in protesting the use of 'sabetsugo' since the 1920s and were the prime movers of the postwar campaigns against linguistic stereotyping through a strategy of vocal denunciation of offenders. Influenced by their evident successes and in many cases actively supported by the BLL, others found their voices during the postwar period, in particular the 1970s and 1980s, as we shall see. But first, a look at the issues involved.

## Linguistic stereotyping and social identity

We construct identities in large part by assigning to ourselves and to others labels which shape our concepts of who and what we or they are. When we label ourselves (or others), the agency is ours and the results (usually) satisfy us. When the agency rests with someone else, the experience may be different. The label might be one with which we are happy to concur; on the other hand, it could be a label we consider demeans and diminishes us. When labels of this latter kind are assigned, the name often focuses on some variation from what is considered the social norm: sexual orientation, perhaps, or race/ethnicity or physical appearance. The intent is to hurt or to dismiss, either actively by hurling an epithet or a stereotype at the intended mark or by perpetuating a casual unthinking slur long ingrained through habit. Not even the youngest child in a playground believes the old saw about 'sticks and stones may break my bones, but names will never hurt me'.

Assigning labels to others plays a significant contrapuntal role in building our own concepts of self. By defining others as what we are not, we emphasize what it is that we think we are, at both personal and social level, often without actually spelling it out. When a society apportions particular names to certain of its members, it reinforces its own belief in what kind of society it is through highlighting in language what it sees as the roles of those members in relation to the whole. This usually serves to label minority groups in such a way as to mark them out as undesirably different from the mainstream:

> Labeling traditions imprison users of language in conventional categories that tend to disallow racial and cultural mixing, to nourish obsessions with purity, and otherwise to help condition visceral ambivalencies about belonging to a disparaged group. Traditional ethnic labels thus discourage the formation of attitudes free of the need to resolve real or fictitious multiple identities into one favored identity.
>
> (Wetherall 1981: 290)

Using negative terms is one way to constitute an undesirable Other. Closely related is defining by exclusion: mainstream society decides the names for 'outsiders within' (Valentine 1998: 3.3), thereby defining by exclusion what is included. In Japan, the nature of mainstream identity is very clearly spelled out in the essentialist Nihonjinron literature (theories of what it means to be Japanese) which has been an influential publishing genre since at least the 1960s. Succinctly put, a 'real' Japanese belongs to the group – i.e. is the same as everybody else in race, language, ethnicity, physical characteristics and cultural heritage. Japan is claimed to be a homogeneous and harmonious society, a construct which leaves very little room for toleration of difference and in effect often denies the existence of marginalized groups. In 2004, acceptance of the idea of multiculturalism appears to be slowly growing in some quarters as a result of the social activism of marginalized groups since the 1980s around the world and of the 1990s' influx of foreign workers. While ethnic diversity is recognized among immigrants, however, the host society is still very much seen as homogeneous. The 'uchi' (insider)/ 'soto' (outsider) dichotomy remains alive and well; public discourse about 'insiders' – i.e. in this instance the Japanese people themselves – gives little or no recognition of internal diversity.

4

If we look at Japan's 'outsiders within', we see that by that process of exclusion the mainstream Japanese is not Burakumin, not Ainu, not of non-Japanese ethnicity, not female, not physically or mentally disabled in any way, and not gay. In other words, he is Japanese of a recognized status and occupation, male, heterosexual, and in good mental and physical health. No marginality here to challenge or cause unease through difference. The reality, however, is quite different. Sugimoto (2003: 1), analysing relevant statistics, concluded that a 'typical' Japanese (i.e. most representative of trends in today's Japan) would be 'a female, non-unionized and non-permanent employee in a small business without university education'. Mainstream identity itself is in reality as diverse as minority identity. 'Identities of minorities are never unified and can exist only in unstable, debatable form within its vaguely determined boundaries *vis-à-vis* the majority. By the same token, identity of the so-called majority is never stable or single: the constitution of majority-ness is often as contested as that of minority-ness' (Ryang 1997: 245).

Sugimoto's findings are certainly not reflected in the language, where the structures of historical inequality, patriarchy and racism can clearly be seen. The stereotyped representations of members of minority groups and the language used to indicate their exclusion are intimately involved with the maintenance of the carefully constructed national identity. Narramore (1997: 42) notes that in Japan's handling of key regional issues, 'the state shows a persistent concern to preserve an homogeneous construction of Japanese identity . . . at a domestic political level this is likely to predominate over a politics of rights'. Where a politics of rights is operational within Japan, he suggests, 'it reinforces an homogeneous construction of Japanese identity'.

We can see this in action in a roundabout way in the effect of the BLL's language protest activities. So effective has been the self-censorship practised by mainstream print and visual media in referring to Burakumin as a result of public denunciations that there is now virtual silence on the topic rather than the wider but more fairly nuanced discussion on discrimination the BLL had hoped to stimulate. The model runs thus: tacitly agreed social silence surrounds Burakumin; someone makes a derogatory reference (not necessarily always referring to Burakumin directly, but involving perhaps a metaphorical comparison); the group carries out a denunciation resulting (most times) in retraction; the silence is then reinforced by media self-censorship for fear of further embarrassment (see Figure 1.1). Result: the homogeneous model of state identity remains untroubled

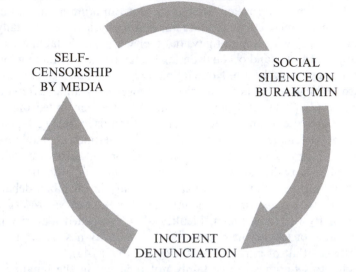

*Figure 1.1* The circular model of Burakumin protest and its effects.

by public reference to uncomfortable realities and acknowledgement of difference. In this respect, then, the confrontational tactics have been counterproductive.

## Language and discrimination: the nexus

Who decides, and on what grounds, whether a term is discriminatory? The answer is clearly those at whom the slur is aimed. To those who have not been the butt of linguistic slurs such decisions may at times seem arbitrary, absurd or rooted in historical events since laundered by time. Letters to newspaper editors often voice reactions of this kind: those who complain about derogatory terms 'can't take a joke', 'have no sense of humour' or need to 'get a life'. Decisions on whether certain language can be regarded as discriminatory are of course made at personal as well as political or corporate levels, with as many views on the subject as there are activists. Power is always a significant factor in the equation. On the one hand, those who use the disputed terms about others wield power – or think they do – over the sense of self and public image of the others through a politics of exclusion and/or denigration. On the other, those who decide that certain words, phrases or stereotypical depictions are discriminatory and therefore should not be used in public discourse exercise power over the language of public life to a certain extent. Agency remains the key.

Arguments about language often hinge on the twin pillars of intent and humour. For every person who argues that a word or phrase is discriminatory, another will retort that it depends on what the person using it intended – perhaps they were unaware that it was a contested term – or that it was 'only a joke'. The humour argument is often heard in Australia and the United Kingdom and, to a lesser extent, the United States. In Australia, normal social discourse in some sections of the community involves making offensive comments to someone in a sardonic way not intended to be taken literally, with 'can't you take a joke?' a common response to a recipient who protests. A recent instance which illustrates this use of 'pejorative endearments' occurred in 2003 over the name of the E.S. 'Nigger' Brown football stand at the Toowoomba Sports Ground in Queensland. It may seem impossible to argue for circumstances in which the word 'nigger' is used by white people without intent to demean. The stance taken by the TSG Trust members, however, was that the particular 1920s sportsman and later civic leader after whom the stand is named was nicknamed 'nigger' because of his fair colouring, with the same ironic sense of humour seen in Virgin Blue's decision to fly red planes on Australian routes ('blue' being a nickname often given to red-haired men). The term dated from that period, they argued, and involves no disrespect to indigenous people. Certain indigenous people living in the area, however, disagreed. Aboriginal activist Stephen Hagan took a complaint to the UN Committee on the Elimination of Racial Discrimination (UNCERD). The Australian government's stance on the matter was that the context in which the nickname was given and is now used on the stand's signage rendered the word 'nigger' inoffensive. UNCERD disagreed and backed Hagan's view, to no avail.

This is not a factor in Japan. The BLL has decided that in the case of their own equivalent to 'nigger', the word 'eta' (sneeringly used to describe their ancestors in the pre-modern period and later, and written with two characters meaning 'great filth'), there are no circumstances which would render the use of this word permissible. Kaneko, taking issue with the use of out of date discriminatory terms in western scholarship on Japan, reflects that a western scholar's use of the word 'eta' to describe people in modern Japan is akin to using 'nigger' as a 'scholarly term' to refer to the Afro-American population in the United States today (1981: 117). Not only that particular

7

term, but all words reflecting in any way poorly on members of Burakumin communities come under the same umbrella.

The language of discrimination cannot, of course, be considered in isolation from its social context. We cannot disaggregate it from the structures of discrimination, neglect and ostracism which it both reflects and constitutes. Doyle (1998: 150–1), speaking of sexist language but in an argument that can equally well be applied to any kind of derogatory language, sums up the two views on this aspect of language:

> Many people believe that discrimination in society will not change simply by ridding our language of sexism. In this view, using non-sexist language is only paying lip-service to reform rather than addressing the very real problems of sexism in society, including discrimination, harassment, violence against women, and economic inequality. Furthermore, in this view, efforts to adopt non-sexist language can be harmful because they can provide a superficially progressive veneer for an organisation while masking its systemic sexism. Others believe that using non-sexist language is an essential part of tackling societal sexism. In this view, language influences our attitudes and behaviour; watching our language goes hand in hand with being careful how we treat others.

'Watching our language' extends in some countries to legislature that makes racial vilification a punishable offence (e.g. Australia's Racial Hatred Act of 1995). Other countries have no such legislation, although redress for personal slander is possible through their defamation laws. Does the lack of a specific law relating to racial vilification send a message that individual freedom of speech takes precedence over an individual's right not to be vilified? Japan has no laws of this kind, despite the urging of UNCERD. Freedom of expression, as provided for in Article 21 of the Constitution, is the major sticking point to Japan's acting on Article 4 of the UNCERD convention (1969, acceded to by Japan in 1996), which stipulates the enactment of legislation outlawing dissemination of racially discriminatory ideas and racially discriminatory acts. The government's position is that Japan will 'fulfil obligations stipulated in article 4 of the Convention so long as they do not contradict the guarantees of the Constitution of Japan'; 'to control all such practices with criminal laws and regulations beyond the current legal system is likely to be contrary to the freedom of expression and other freedoms guaranteed by the Constitution' (CERD 2000a: paragraph 74). Article 4 of UNCERD states that:

States Parties condemn all propaganda and all organizations which are based on ideas or theories of superiority of one race or group of persons of one colour or ethnic origin, or which attempt to justify or promote racial hatred and discrimination in any form, and undertake to adopt immediate and positive measures designed to eradicate all incitement to, or acts of, such discrimination and, to this end, with due regard to the principles embodied in the Universal Declaration of Human Rights and the rights expressly set forth in article 5 of this Convention, inter alia:

(a) Shall declare *an offence punishable by law* [my italics] all dissemination of ideas based on racial superiority or hatred, incitement to racial discrimination, as well as all acts of violence or incitement to such acts against any race or group of persons of another colour or ethnic origin, and also the provision of any assistance to racist activities, including the financing thereof;

(b) Shall declare illegal and prohibit organizations, and also organized and all other propaganda activities, which promote and incite racial discrimination, and shall recognize participation in such organizations or activities as an offence punishable by law;

(c) Shall not permit public authorities or public institutions, national or local, to promote or incite racial discrimination.

(Office of the High Commissioner for
Human Rights 1969)

Japan's periodic reports to CERD, the Convention's monitoring body, have been criticized for the failure to enact the law required by Article 4. Japan's first and second periodic reports, for example, submitted together in 1999, argued that Article 14 of its Constitution ('all of the people are equal under the law and there shall be no discrimination in political, economic or social relations because of race, creed, sex, social status or family origin') is sufficient to guarantee equality before the law without enacting a racial discrimination law which would conflict with freedom of expression.

9

Pointing out that other avenues existed under the Penal Code for punishing various consequences of discriminatory conduct, the report summed up the Japanese position thus:

> The Government believes that respect of human rights by the general public should be essentially enhanced through free speech guaranteed by the right to freedom of expression, and that it is most appropriate that a society itself eliminate any existing discrimination and prejudice of its own will by respecting the constitutional provision prohibiting the abuse of freedom and rights. It is hoped that public relations activities conducted by the Government will facilitate such a self-cleansing action in the society.
>
> (CERD 2000a: paragraph 75)

Then follows a long description of the sorts of 'educational' activities instituted by officers of the Civil Liberties Bureau of the Ministry of Justice following a rash of incidents of harassment of Korean students in 1998; a description of the organizational structure for protecting human rights through investigation and education (but only if the offender agrees to participate); and a couple of examples involving discrimination against foreigners and the manner in which they had been resolved.

The Committee's response indicated that it was unimpressed by these arguments. Requesting a full breakdown on the ethnic composition of the population of Japan, omitted from the periodic report on the grounds of being too difficult, the Committee noted that Japan's refusal to implement a specific law left it in contravention of the Convention. The response paper argued that 'article 4 is of mandatory nature, given the non-self-executing character of all its provisions, and the prohibition of the dissemination of all ideas based upon racial superiority or hatred is compatible with the rights to freedom of opinion and expression' (CERD 2000b: para. 11). The actions undertaken in the case of the anti-Korean incidents referred to above were deemed inadequate and the government was urged to act more resolutely in future. Legislation ought to be introduced whereby instances of racial discrimination could be made subject to penalty and public officials should be trained in human rights issues to avoid the kind of discriminatory pronouncements that had recently been made by high-level public officials without attracting subsequent sanction from the authorities. Burakumin were not to be excluded from protection against discrimination as outlined in Article 1 of the Convention on the grounds that they were of the same race as other Japanese; 'descent' was in their case a salient reason for including them in anti-discrimination measures.

To date the third and fourth period reports of Japan, due in January 2003, in which these issues were to have been addressed, have not been submitted, as far as I can ascertain, and by the end of the 159th ordinary session of the Diet (Japanese Parliament) in June 2004 no progress had been made towards the implementation of legislation outlawing racial discrimination. The BLL has been active in agitating for such a law for years: the most recent issue of the online *Buraku Liberation News* contained an article outlining a draft, prepared by the BLL, of what such a bill might look like (Matsuoka 2004). However, no substantial progress has yet been made towards the realization of such a law.

## Media responses

Where no legislation exists, complaints from individuals are unlikely to bring about change or provide redress. The most effective way for complainants to present their case is likely to be a group approach from, say, disability support organizations or Chinese community groups over language use in public fora. Certainly that has been the trajectory followed in Japan: the only regulation of contested language use that has occurred over the last 30 or 40 years has come about through media self-regulation following such protests and not through legal channels. Japan's National Language Council, up to and subsequent to its downgrading in 2001 to a sub-committee of the Cultural Affairs Committee, did not ever involve itself in the debate over discriminatory language; thus, no policy position exists on this issue in the language policy literature. In any case, such a position, were it to be prescriptive, would more appropriately belong in the domain of law rather than language management *per se*, where it could only ever be admonitory.

The concerted efforts of various organizations representing minorities have achieved notable success in influencing – some would say muzzling – the Japanese media since the 1970s, to the extent that the media is now to a large degree its own best watchdog in terms of what language it uses. Each major media organization has developed a list of terms to be avoided, usually called a 'kinkushū' (list of forbidden terms) or 'iikaeshū' (list of substitute expressions). A few are public, such as that of the Japan Broadcasting Corporation

11

(NHK), the national public broadcaster; others are in-house. Not all companies will admit to the existence of the lists; so sensitive did the issue become that by the time representatives from the *Yomiuri* and *Mainichi* newspapers were interviewed by a researcher in 1994, they revealed that they could not admit to having such guidelines even though they actually did. Criticisms of 'kotobagari' (language hunts) caused by revealing that they had such lists were considered almost as embarrassing as the glare of unwelcome publicity caused by denunciations if they did not (Sukigara 1995). A code of silence – which nevertheless does nothing to stop the public knowing that these lists exist – thus often prevails. Input from the general public into decisions about the words on the list has been minimal or non-existent; the decisions have been made in-house and not generally communicated outside. Where a protest has been made about language used in a print publication, the next issue of that publication generally carries an apology. On TV, shows are occasionally interrupted with a message along the lines of 'we apologize for inadvertently using an inappropriate term in Programme X the other day', and broadcasts of older films are often sprinkled with hissing or buzzing noises where words considered inappropriate in today's context are beeped out.

One argument that could be mounted against this is that the press are in fact putting a lot of effort into the wrong thing. Although public appearances of discriminatory terms are now restricted mostly to toilet walls or graffiti in parks, and of course on the internet, rather than in the mass media, social discrimination itself has not appreciably decreased as a result. If words have no more than a symbolic connection to what they represent, then regulating their use does nothing to improve the underlying situation. Banning the words will not remove the prejudice which produces them, and may in fact only increase it. If, on the other hand, language is seen as constructing reality, then sanitizing certain terms might indeed have an effect, at least in terms of perceptions if not of infrastructural changes; the change in perceptions would then in time lead to infrastructural improvements for the group concerned. Media organizations in this latter case could be argued to be working towards the eradication of attitudinal discrimination by removing contested language from public discourse. But this has not been the case at all in Japan: as we shall see in more detail later on, the primary motivation for developing editorial regulation of language was to avoid the public embarrassment of vocal protests in a society where face is all-important.

Media language plays a pivotal role in determining public attitudes and perceptions. Any decision by media organizations to discontinue the use of certain kinds of words might therefore be thought likely to have an influence on public perceptions one way or the other (assuming the public is made aware of the decision and the reasons behind it). Japan, of course, is not the only country where lists have been drawn up. In direct response to social movements seeking redress for the marginalization of citizens on the grounds of race, ethnicity, gender and disability, many major media companies, government departments and universities in English-speaking countries such as the United Kingdom, the United States and Australia began to produce – and still produce – guidelines on terms to be avoided on the grounds that minority groups find them offensive. In Australia, for example, where multiculturalism, Aboriginal reconciliation, feminism and disability rights movements have contributed to shaping social debate since the 1970s, various government departments[1] have put in place guidelines for using non-discriminatory language in the public sector.

Japan has the world's largest number of daily newspapers, many of which put out both morning and evening editions. Total newspaper circulation in 2002 was over 71 million, compared with over 55 million in the United States and nearly 18 million in Britain (Nikkei 2003b). A comparison of major Japanese and British broadsheets for the same period shows that the circulation of the top five broadsheets combined in Japan at this time worked out to one copy per 4.6 people, compared to one copy for 25.7 people in Britain (Nikkei 2003a). In addition to radio networks, Japan has over 200 TV stations; a survey in 2000 reported a national daily average viewing time of around three and a half hours (Kamimura *et al.* 2003). The kind of language used in the press and in broadcasting is thus very important. Given the size of the newspaper industry, the number of hours spent watching TV each day and the reach of the radio, media language reaches and influences most people in the course of their daily lives. The role of the editor as gatekeeper in influencing which forms will be adopted and therefore sanctioned (Romaine 1999: 311) or, conversely, not used, is crucial.

The code of ethics of the National Association of Commercial Broadcasters in Japan, *Broadcasting Standards*, last revised in 1999, is somewhat short on specifics in its approach to language use. In Section 8, devoted to 'Consideration for Expressions', we find exhortations to avoid obscenity, to handle with care material whose content might upset audiences, to present multifaceted views where

13

topics may be controversial, and a host of other references to handling material of different sorts in a manner calculated not to upset
people. Item 56 states that 'in the handling of matters related to
mental or physical handicap, the feelings of those who suffer such
conditions shall be carefully considered'. No concrete guidance is
offered, however, as to what this actually entails. Print media organizations are more forthright and forthcoming, specifying in annual
publications such as the *Kisha Handobukku* (*Journalists' Handbook*)
which words ought to be avoided and what should be used in their
place. Reporters are advised that certain words and expressions
related to status, illness, gender, occupation, race, ethnicity and
locale are not used because they express discriminatory attitudes,
and because reporters have a responsibility to do their best to
protect basic human rights and stamp out discrimination (Kyōdō
Tsūshinsha 1999: 82).

The Yōgo to Sabetsu o kangaeru Shinpojiumu Jikkō Iinkai
(Executive Committee of the Symposium on Language and Discrimination) consisted of representatives from publishing, broadcasting, press, writers, performing arts and disability support groups.
Between 1975 and 1989 it produced three editions of a substantial
book tracking the progress of the debate, listing and discussing
examples of denunciations and self-censorship reactions, providing the minutes of their meetings and public discussions, and printing examples of the self-censorship lists used by certain companies.
Although the 1970s saw a spate of newspaper editorials and columns, and of special issues of periodicals devoted to the debate,
most carefully avoided any reference to Burakumin issues, concentrating instead on words relating to people with disabilities or on
the self-censorship lists themselves (Yōgo to Sabetsu o kangaeru
Shinpojiumu Jikkō Iinkai 1989: 5). It is this body's publications which
openly confirm what many cynically averred, that it was specifically
in order to avoid being denounced by the BLL that the 'iikaeshū'
and 'kinkushū' were developed by mass media company managers
in addition to letters of apology, seeking to avoid 'friction' by 'self-
regulation'. In companies producing textbooks, teachers with links
to the BLL had input into the text before publication.

In September 1973, the National Association of Private Broadcasters in Japan circulated to its member companies a document
entitled *Sabetsu Yōgo to Kyūdan Rei* (*Examples of Discriminatory
Language and Denunciations*), following an initial 'warning' three
months earlier. The document noted that although most of the earlier
incidents had occurred in the Osaka area they were now spreading

14

to Tokyo, and that the BLL decision to pursue the mass media had proven a very effective strategy for fostering a general understanding of 'dōwa mondai' (Burakumin issues). What broadcasters should do, in order to avoid the damage accruing from lengthy denunciation sessions, was *inter alia* take care to warn guest stars on programmes to be careful what they said (since many incidents had resulted from pronouncements by artists), and make sure that discriminatory terms referring to Burakumin were never used. The thrust of the document was that it was the guest stars, not the station, who were responsible for slip-ups, and that since the BLL were bound to be vocal about it, it was best to avoid unnecessary friction (Yōgo to Sabetsu o kangaeru Shinpojiumu Jikkō Iinkai 1989: 24–5).

That saw the beginning of a rush by other bodies to produce their own regulations, starting with a confidential document from Japanese TV station TBS in 1973 called *Hōsōjo saketai Kotoba* (*Language to be Avoided in Broadcasting*). Each company's handbook was virtually the same as all the others, as companies exchanged information at the monthly meeting of the Terminology Discussion Group of the Japan Newspaper Publishers and Editors Association. As NHK and the major commercial broadcasters also participated in these meetings, this mode of response to complaints spread widely, with the further inclusion in the lists of words relating to disability and occupation as well as to Burakumin. Implementation became mandatory; regardless of whether the words were used as part of a historical drama or in older programmes and films, they were cut. Specialist staff nervously monitored live broadcasts and inserted an apology and correction if any mishap occurred (Yōgo to Sabetsu o kangaeru Shinpojiumu Jikkō Iinkai 1989: 26).

In order to know which specific words are avoided, we must examine the lists used in media organizations and the advice given in the *Kisha Handobukku*. As in most fields of human endeavour, the urge to codify and quantify is strong once an issue has been identified. Books such as Takagi (1999) and Yōgo to Sabetsu o kangaeru Shinpojiumu Jikkō Iinkai (1989) include several lists, some of them otherwise unpublished (e.g. a 1994 *Asahi Shimbun* document, one from Mainichi Broadcasting, the *Yomiuri* stylebook and so on). Several lists can also be found online. Some of these, linked to personal homepages, prove ephemeral, but in December 2004 online collections could be found at http://home.att.ne.jp/wood/micci/WandC/TABOO.htm, www.jekai.org/entries/aa/00/np/aa00np30.htm and http://kan-chan.stbbs.net/word/pc/list.txt.

Terms specific to discrimination based on status, ethnicity, disability and gender will be discussed in detail in the following chapters, but broadly, the lists and style sheets adopt the following classifications of terms to avoid:

1 People and human rights (e.g. buraku [segregated hamlet], tokushu buraku [special hamlet], mimoto chōsa [background checks]).
2 Physical or mental features (e.g. mekura [blind], tsunbo [deaf], oshi [mute], hakuchi [idiot]).
3 Occupation (e.g. inugoroshi [dog killer], kuzuya [junkman], onbō [crematorium worker]).
4 Particular countries, people and races (e.g. kuronbo [black person], jappu [Jap], Shina [contested term for China]).
5 Words which upset people or make them feel uncomfortable (e.g. onnakodomo [women and children] and other gender-related terms, unko [shit]).

Each of the documents is company-specific (or profession-specific in the case of the *Kisha Handobukku*), and some go into much greater detail than others.

To give some examples: the 1974 NHK programme standards handbook (excerpted in Yōgo to Sabetsu o kangaeru Shinpojiumu Jikkō Iinkai 1989: 307–23) divided the terms into several categories, among them those pertaining to human rights, character and reputation/dignity, and race, ethnicity and international relations. The first of these was prefaced by three guiding principles: that human rights would be protected and character respected; that no broadcasts would be made which injure the reputation of individuals or groups and damage confidence in them; and that discriminatory references to occupations would be avoided. This category encompassed references to people with physical or mental disabilities, slighting references to certain occupations, such as those of servant or manual labourer, and references to Burakumin. The principles to be observed when reporting on the second category (race, ethnicity and international relations) were that broadcasts should not give rise to racial or ethnic prejudice or interfere with friendly international relations. Slighting references to particular racial or ethnic names, customs or languages were to be avoided, and the use of humour in these areas was to be carefully monitored.

The eleventh section of the handbook, dealing with occupations, lists particular terms to be avoided, offering alternative ways of expressing the same meanings. Job descriptions such as 'inugoroshi' (dog killer) and 'onbō' (cremator) were to be replaced with the less emotive 'yaken hokakuin' and 'kasō sagyōin' respectively; 'kuronbo' (blacks) and 'ketō' (whites) with 'kokujin' and 'hakujin'; 'kozukai' (servant, janitor) with 'yōmuin'. References to blind, deaf and lame people were changed to 'me/mimi/ashi no fujiyū na . . .', and so on. In addition, a list of pejorative or vulgar terms to be avoided was included, for example, 'himo' (adulterer, paramour) would be replaced with 'jōfu', 'mae' (priors) with 'zenka' (criminal record), 'uranihon' (the back of Japan) with 'Nihonkai-gawa' (the Japan Sea side), and 'kōshinkoku' (a backward country) with 'hatten tojōkoku' (developing country).

The following year, the *Asahi Shimbun* developed its own set of guidelines (Yōgo to Sabetsu o kangaeru Shinpojiumu Jikkō Iinkai 1989: 324–6), also premised on the basic principle of the protection of human rights. Due care and attention, the preamble warned, must be paid to what was termed 'discriminatory language' referring to groups such as the Burakumin and the disabled; journalists must learn to see things from the point of view of those vulnerable to discrimination and must realize that even the casual use of certain terms could cause pain regardless of whether the journalist had intended no harm in using them. The usual terms relating to occupations, nationalities and disabilities were listed along with suggested substitutions, some slightly different from those given by NHK: 'mōjin' or 'me ga mienai hito' were to be used instead of 'mekura', for example, and 'ashi no warui hito' and 'ashi no fujiyū na hito' instead of 'bikko/chinba/izari'. 'Tokushu buraku' was to be replaced with 'hisabetsu buraku' (discriminated-against hamlets), 'mikaihō buraku' (unliberated hamlets) or 'dōwa chiku'. Where the word 'buraku' itself simply indicated 'a hamlet community' (i.e. non-Burakumin), it should be changed to 'shūraku' or 'chiku' so as not to give the reader the impression that it referred to a Burakumin community. Certain words relating to marital status or age were to be revised, for example, 'mekake' (mistress), 'nigō' (number two, = mistress) and 'jōfu' (mistress) were all to be replaced by 'koibito' (lover); 'rōba' (old hag) by 'rōjo' or 'rōfujin' (old woman); and words such as 'demodori' (divorce) and 'ōrudomisu' (old maid) were to be avoided.

Other organizations' guidelines (those of the *Mainichi* and *Yomiuri* newspapers and some regional newspapers, also excerpted in Yōgo to Sabetsu o kangaeru Shinpojiumu Jikkō Iinkai 1989) followed similar principles; despite some slight differences in coverage all encompassed

17

the broad areas relating to race and ethnicity, social status and health differences. Private sector TV took the lead from NHK: the 1985 revised version of the TV Asahi guidelines on terms to be used in broadcasting lists terms which 'depending on how they are used, may cause distress by unfairly discriminating against or insulting people'. The list is divided into five sections dealing with race/ethnicity/ nationality, Burakumin, occupations, people with disabilities and 'other' (which included reference to concepts of privacy).

The guidelines for various publishers and media are all different because they are not regulated by any overarching law; thus, what may be forbidden by one station is accepted by another, for example, Chiba Terebi permits 'kobito' (dwarf), while Nihon Terebi does not and cuts it from films. In many cases media have instantly caved in to suggestions that a word might be discriminatory and have banned it after just one protest, without further investigation (Hanagoyomi FAQ, http://kan-chan.stbbs.net/word/pc/faq.html). A contributor to the discussion group on the same website in 2001 reported asking for help in finding the views of the Ministry of Education on discriminatory language relating to Ainu, other ethnic minorities and women, and being told that the Ministry had no views, it being not a matter of law but rather a matter of media choice that certain words were not used. In both cases the influence of the media in censoring language is unquestioned.

Fasold's examination of language policy relating to sexist language in US periodicals and newspapers concluded that 'success [in such types of language planning] is increased if the plan is directed at written rather than spoken usage, involves a limited scope of application, does not exceed enforcement capabilities, and is not overly innovative' (1987: 203). In the Japanese case, however, the remit is much broader: both written material (except as yet for that appearing on the internet, although that is beginning to change) and spoken language in films, radio broadcasts and TV shows are scrutinized. Spoken language, by virtue of its immediacy, is less easy to police, as shown by the protests occasioned from time to time by the utterances of guests on interview programmes who are not aware of the broadcaster's language conventions. Such incidents are always followed by an apology from the broadcaster and an admission that the language had been inappropriate. While there have been protests in other countries about media language, they have not reached the scale and ferocity of some of the denunciations carried out in Japan, which explains the eagerness of the media to extend caution to the spoken as well as written word.

Almost 15 years ago, Fasold *et al.* (1990: 538) were optimistic that the US press would ultimately attain gender equity in reporting:

Although there seems to be a long way to go before news reporting is entirely equitable along gender lines, there has also been measurable progress. Since newspapers are read by millions of people daily, and since the editorial policies of newspapers seem to have considerable effect, it might seem that this would be a good place to exert pressure for further progress.

In Japan, although the language restrictions are upheld by editors, it became clear during the process of this research that they in large part incite derision from the public (those who are aware of their existence, at least). Certainly internet discussion groups tend to treat them in this way. Despite the indisputable potential for media language to influence attitudes, therefore, whether or not such language restrictions are viewed with respect has a part to play in the manner in which the reader receives that text. Whether such measures have any chance of fostering change or not depends on what their aim is perceived to be. People who view themselves as free from prejudiced attitudes are likely to maintain a healthy cynicism towards what they might see as language manipulation; at the same time, overtly prejudiced people are unlikely to be convinced (in the immediate short term, at least) to modify their attitudes by the substitution of innocuous terms for derogatory ones.

The main aim of the regulations in Japan, despite the introductory statements about respect for human rights which preface the lists, is to protect the media from public embarrassment arising from complaints or more active protests. Much of what many feel is media over-self-censorship stems directly from fear of the BLL's language protests and denunciations which were occasionally violent and always confrontational (Tajima *et al.* 1998: 110). Valentine (1997: 58), for instance, remarks on the role played by fear of complaint in avoiding outright discriminatory representations on Japanese TV of people with disabilities or from marginalized ethnic groups, though other stereotyping still occurs. A self-directed motive of this kind, however, does nothing to address the discriminatory attitudes underlying the offensive language and the lists are thus little more than a cosmetic solution which conceals the real dimensions of discrimination.

A similar phenomenon has been encountered in state attempts to provide solutions for people with disabilities: 'the goal is not to address the needs of the disabled, but to make it *look* as if those needs are being met'. By putting (unsuccessful) raised bumps on currency bills, the government and Japanese without disabilities are able to feel as if they are being inclusive, whereas the measure does not work as intended at all (Nakamura 2002: 19). Similarly with media self-censorship: the attempt to avoid embarrassment not to the people of whom derogatory words are used but to the media against which retribution will be directed enables the organizations involved to say that they are addressing the problem, whereas in reality they are not.

> Where people can cause trouble, calling names may become a matter of concern, in which pretensions to care about the discriminated often derive from consideration of the self-image of the discriminator. This concern may lead to euphemistic substitution or to denial of reference if naming the other is deemed to cause more trouble than it is worth.
>
> (Valentine 1998: 5.7)

This succinctly summarizes what has happened in the case of the Burakumin. While the 'kyūdan' (denunciation) policy has put a stop to discriminatory stereotyping in the media and public documents, it has also virtually muzzled open discussion of Burakumin issues because that is seen as likely to be more trouble than it is worth. Given that 'media discourse is the main source of people's knowledge, attitudes and ideologies' (Van Dijk 2000: 36–7), this silence is counterproductive as far as educating the public about the realities of discrimination through the press is concerned.

Responses to Burakumin language protests since the late 1970s have been classified into three broad types: positive acceptance of the substance of a complaint and an attempt to find new ways of talking about Burakumin issues; emergency evasive measures on receipt of a complaint; and criticism of the complaint itself, after which people continue to do as they wish, citing freedom of speech as their justification. The 'iikaeshū' fall into the second of these categories – i.e. they are emergency measures taken to avert criticism and to paper over a difficult issue rather than coming to grips with the substantive matters of discrimination which lie behind the complaints (Kawamoto 1995: 46–7). In other words, their main aim is to save face.

The urge to save face is understandable, given the tactics to which they might otherwise be subjected. An interesting glimpse into how media intimidation works is offered (in a different context) by David McNeill, who describes his experience with a right-wing nationalist group whose members took exception to a comment he made about the Nanjing massacre during a broadcast. The group threatened the station management that if no public apology was made on air they would harass the programme's sponsors into withdrawing their support by continually driving their sound trucks past their business premises. Management reacted not by rejecting the demand but by immediately requesting McNeill to apologize and also to desist from all further discussion of political affairs. Musing on what makes Japanese media so willing to comply with intimidation of this kind, McNeill (2001) observes that the usual explanation – that social constructs of group-centred consensus seek compromise aimed at maintaining harmony –

is superficially plausible but fails to explain where this drive comes from or what interests might be served by it . . . This notion of consensus, reinforced through the education system and other state apparatus, often boils down, in practice, to the imposition of power over dissenting, minority, and sometimes even, majority opinion.

The media in Japan limit the agenda rather than setting it as in other countries, as we can see by the virtual silence on Burakumin which leaves no room for that group to contribute to setting the agenda in terms of what is discussed.

Sociologist Fukuoka Yasunori argues that the differentiation between the use of the words 'sabetsugo' and 'sabetsu yōgo' lies in terms of media motivation (Isomura and Fukuoka 1994: 15–50). From 1973 on, he notes, during a period which saw one complaint or denunciation of media organizations after another, those complaining used the term 'sabetsugo' while most media organizations used 'sabetsu yōgo'. Fukuoka defines 'sabetsugo' as specific words which, because of their association with instances of real social and historical discrimination, continue to carry negative emotional shades of meaning towards those who have suffered that particular kind of discrimination. The specific instance he uses to illustrate this is the phrase 'tokushu buraku' (special hamlet), coined by late-Meiji bureaucrats to distinguish Burakumin hamlets from other hamlets and continuing, long after its bureaucratic use was discontinued, to carry a connotation of unacceptable difference. The specific functions enacted by 'sabetsugo', Fukuoka posits, are twofold: to hurt the feelings of those of whom they are used and to engender and perpetuate discriminatory attitudes in those who hear them. Even used metaphorically, as has often been the case with 'tokushu buraku', language of this sort demeans the third party to whom it refers, rendering both the user and the hearer (who may angrily deny the comparison) complicit in discriminating against the referent.

'Sabetsu yōgo', on the other hand, is the term favoured by the media post-1973 when they drew up 'kinkushū' and 'iikaeshū'. Having scrutinized many such collections, Fukuoka argues that while all such in-house lists claim respect for human rights as their guiding principle, in reality the underlying motivation – as made clear by the wording of the prefaces – is to avoid 'trouble' in the form of public protests. This is a clear-cut case of one of Japan's ideological binary oppositions, 'tatemae' and 'honne', at work: while the 'tatemae' (official position) is that human rights must be protected, the 'honne' (real underlying motive) is to escape the personal embarrassment of being subjected to public protest rather than to advance altruistic social goals. Such an approach reveals that while media organizations may be aware of the first function of 'sabetsugo' noted above, namely its power to wound the referent, they are insufficiently alive to its second function of perpetuating discriminatory attitudes: what McConnell-Ginet (1998: 199) refers to as 'the significance of the tagging process itself and the possibility that this process shapes and gives coherence to the sometimes inchoate stuff that we seek to wrap our tags around'. The media lists do not provide any detailed explanation of *why* each word on the list is discriminatory, strengthening the impression that they are merely kneejerk reactions to confrontation handed down from on high to journalists with instructions not to use those words. The guidelines are then applied mechanically, without any real effort to understand the underlying issues. Fukuoka relates anecdotal evidence of being shown one such in-house document where a word relating to Koreans was banned solely on the grounds that a complaint had been received, with no reflection at all on the issue involved.

In the context of non-sexist language, Cameron (1998: 159–61) also takes up this point:

> Denying that your guidelines have any particular agenda only means that you will not be able to make a convincing argument for preferring them to the alternatives . . . The

crucial aspect of language is meaning: the point of non-sexist language is not to change the forms of words for the sake of it but to change the repertoire of meanings a language conveys. It's about redefining rather than merely renaming the world.

In Japan there were never any political intentions, overt or otherwise, behind the media guidelines on language. Far from making media organizations appear progressive and enlightened, as we have seen, the guidelines are widely viewed as a cynical and pragmatic reaction to external pressure, although to those whose complaints have resulted in their establishment they are of course much more than that. And yet, regardless of the real underlying motive for having such lists, they do perform a service in that by provoking discussion on their existence they challenge the belief that the meanings of words are fixed and transparent and that this is 'how things are' in that society.

I conclude this chapter with a quote from Van Dijk (2000: 36–7), who notes that 'the media elites are ultimately responsible for the prevailing discourses of the media they control. This is specifically also true for the role of the media in ethnic affairs, for the following reasons'. He lists nine reasons, of which I reproduce here those most relevant to Japan, replacing the word 'white' with 'Japanese':

- Most Japanese readers have few daily experiences with minorities.
- Most Japanese readers have few alternative sources for information about minorities.
- Negative attitudes about minorities are in the interests of most Japanese readers.
- More than most other topics, ethnic issues provide positive but polarized identification for most Japanese readers, in terms of us-and-them (true, particularly in reports linking increases in crime to foreigners).
- The media emphasize such group polarization by focusing on various Problems and Threats for Us, thus actively involving most Japanese readers (true).
- Minority groups do not have enough power to publicly oppose biased reporting.

All except the last of these is true in the case of Japan. Negative attitudes to minorities are certainly in the interest of maintaining the fiction of the 'pure' national identity, and newspaper reports have

23

often linked rising crime rates with foreign elements. It is certainly not the case, however, that in Japan minority groups do not have enough power to publicly oppose biased reporting: some have wielded sufficient power to bring about media self-regulation in reporting on their issues. Language relating to smaller ethnic minority groups, however, may not have been regulated as readily had it not been for the example of the pulling power of the larger groups, specifically the BLL.

# 2

# THE FLOW-ON EFFECTS

We saw in the previous chapter that media language relating to minority groups has been regulated on a voluntary basis since the 1970s, but that public perceptions of this regulation are largely cynical, given that it is based on a desire to avoid potentially embarrassing protests rather than having any real aim of decreasing discriminatory attitudes. In this chapter, we move on to the inevitable backlash that such practices incurred in the 1990s, when discussion of 'political correctness' was brought to the boil by a high-profile writer. The 1990s also saw the resurfacing of discriminatory language in the public arena, on the internet. We examine, too, how dictionaries have responded in part to the changing views of certain terms, in particular those relating to Burakumin.

## 'Kotobagari': Japan's 'political correctness' backlash

As in other countries, the debate on political correctness in Japan took place in the 1990s, a couple of decades after media guidelines on language use were established. Intervention by publishers and editors over the years created a degree of dissatisfaction, particularly among writers, which was brought to a head by an incident involving prominent writer Tsutsui Yasutaka in 1993, when the Japan Epilepsy Association (JEA) protested against the inclusion in a school textbook of one of his short stories which they believed encouraged discrimination against people with epilepsy (see Namase 1994). Although Tsutsui's publisher, Kadokawa, supported him, the author took umbrage at what he termed unacceptable 'kotobagari' (language hunts) and announced that he would give up writing in protest (a decision rescinded several years later). The incident was the catalyst for heated public discussion, with on the one side disability groups supporting the JEA and on the other writers arguing that freedom of speech, and in particular the artistic freedom to write fiction unchallenged, was under threat.

Political correctness (PC) is defined as a label which 'has become a broad brush applied to any effort to reflect our changing society that goes against the status quo' (Doyle 1998: 152) and as a smear term which 'has provided a new pretext for attacking the whole idea of politically motivated linguistic reform' (Cameron 1998: 158). To attack someone using the charge of 'political correctness' is to imply that no attention need be paid to their arguments about language since they are motivated by authoritarian extremism or over-delicate sensibilities. In Japan, the phonetic katakana trans-literation of the English 'political correctness' is occasionally used to refer to PC, but the more usual term is the evocative 'kotobagari' (language hunts), with its connotations of search and destroy. Fear of being accused of 'kotobagari' in the 1990s became another of the reasons why most major media companies do not make public their lists of words.

In Japan as elsewhere, the two most commonly heard argu-ments against regulating language use are that it violates freedom of speech and that it leads to impoverishment of the language (Yōgo to Sabetsu o kangaeru Shinpojiumu Jikkō Iinkai 1989: 4). The word 'kotobagari' is rarely used without the words 'hyōgen no jiyū' (freedom of expression) occurring somewhere nearby. Attempt-ing to shape the way in which public texts such as newspapers and statutes refer to minority group members, it is argued, is not an acknowledgement of the rights and sensitivities of part of society but an infringement of the right to free speech of the whole. This over-looks the fact that there is no such thing as completely free speech in the eyes of the law. If I defame you, you can take me to court. If I swear at a police officer, I can be arrested on that account. If I egg on a lynch mob with cries of 'kill the nigger!', I can be arrested for inciting violence. We are already constrained in our use of speech by the laws which regulate the way in which we live together – i.e. we do not have the right to use language which causes overt harm as a consequence of what we say, either through the ruin of a reputation or possible physical harm and violence to others.

What occurs within the private sphere usually remains private. It is within the public sphere that 'political correctness' is most ferociously challenged. Opinions differ over the point at which the right to speak as we wish (always excepting the examples given above) takes precedence over the effect that such speech, known in the United States as 'hate speech', may have on its target. Hate speech is here defined as 'speech that denigrates persons on the basis of their race or ethnic origin, religion, gender, age, physical condition, disability, sexual orientation, and so forth' (Sedler 1992, cited in Leets 2002). The debate over at what point, if any, there is a role for society to intervene usually focuses on legislation but also encompasses a large literature on 'political correctness'.

With regard to the second charge, that 'kotobagari' leads to impoverishment of the language, Fukuoka argues that those who complain that the Japanese language will be diminished if words are lost as a result of complaints that they are discriminatory have most likely never thought through the issue of whether particular words they themselves use in everyday conversation fulfil the two functions of 'sabetsugo', wounding the referent, and perpetuating discriminatory attitudes (Isomura and Fukuoka 1994: 23). This would seem to imply that only personal experience can contribute to any real understanding of the value of restraint in language. At the same time, however, we ought reasonably to be able to expect that language used without respect for substantial portions of its speakers is open to question from society as a whole. The 'needs' of the abstract concept of the language itself, which is in any case not a static entity but in a constant state of dynamic flux, should not be used to subvert those of its speakers. It is difficult to imagine in what ways a language could be diminished by eliminating the use of words which carry overt historical and discriminatory baggage towards sections of the population, or at least by identifying them as such in dictionaries.

The use of euphemisms has always figured prominently in charges of 'political correctness'. Japanese terms such as 'ashi no fujiyū na kata' for someone unable to walk properly (or at all) are euphemisms for older words such as 'bikko' (cripple), and we shall see in Chapter 5 how a whole stable of such terms was developed during the 1980s in relation to disabilities. Euphemisms, however, well-intended as they may seem, do not necessarily achieve a positive outcome (and of course, they have often been used in the past to indicate objects of discrimination by not naming them directly). Quite apart from the laughter that some of the more over-the-top expressions which were deliberately created as jokes have caused in English-speaking countries, euphemisms are just another form of labelling which may function to exclude just as effectively as the terms they replace, in that they continue to flag difference but this time along whited-sepulchre lines. 'Those who upset the system, and have the power to show up the polite progressive façade, are wrapped in delicate designations that are frequently the province and progeny of experts, whose euphemism may be as disabling as more blatantly discriminatory terms' (Valentine 2002: 218). 'Kusai mono ni futa o shiro' (put a lid on a stink), runs the old Japanese proverb, and that is what many people with disabilities in Japan perceive as having happened. As will be further discussed in Chapter 5, the word 'shōgaisha' itself, commonly used in legal and political documents since the 1980s to indicate a person with a disability, is problematic because of the association of its second component character with harm or damage. Euphemisms themselves have limited life spans: 'since attitudes toward the original referent are not altered by a change of name, the new name itself takes on the adverse connotations, and a new euphemism must be found' (Lakoff 1975: 20; see also Cameron 1995: 145–6).

Euphemisms are facilitated in Japan by the nature of the writing system, where the existence of multiple readings or pronunciations for most characters results in a tendency to use the *on* (Chinese-derived) reading in euphemisms rather than the *kun* (native Japanese) reading. This lends the euphemism a formal tone and deprives it of immediacy, setting it apart to some extent from everyday speech and marking it as a term most likely to be found in formal documents (Valentine 2002: 221–2). Rather than the now contested 'mekura' *kun* reading for the character for 'blind' being used in the phrase 'mekura no hito' (blind person), for example, it is the *on* reading 'mō' which is used in the preferred euphemism of 'mōjin' (same meaning). Visual effects made possible by the existence of both the ideographic kanji and the phonetic hiragana and katakana scripts also contribute: 'Mekura' (now considered a discriminatory term for blind) might be slightly less offensive when written in *hiragana*, rendering the sounds for 'eye' and 'dark', rather than in the *kanji*, that places 'dead' over 'eye' – i.e., めくら rather than 盲.

When I opened my Japanese text input program to insert these characters, I found that the character 盲 would not come up under the reading 'mekura', only with the reading 'mō'. Other contested words which could not be automatically converted included 'eta' and 'hinin', where the characters mean 'great filth' and 'non-human' respectively; these words could only be input in hiragana. 'Shinheimin' (new commoner, i.e. Burakumin) would not convert as a phrase, only with 'shin' and 'heimin' as separate segments. 'Kichigai' (crazy) could not be converted; nor could 'shina', a contested term for China, or several other words related to ethnic discrimination. 'Hakuchi' (idiot), 'raibyō' (leprosy), long since replaced in the word lists by 'Hansen-byō' (Hansen's disease), 'bikko' (lame), 'oshi' (deaf-mute), 'haishitsu' (deformity), 'fugu' (cripple), 'chinba' (lame): none of the words considered out of line for describing disability will automatically convert but must be input by other means if the writer wants to use that word. Longer substitutes such as 'ashi ga fujiyū na hito', 'me ga mienai hito' and 'chiteki shōgaisha', however, come up straight away. The conversion process and the internal dictionaries are clearly designed along the same lines as the 'iikaeshū' (see Gottlieb 1995 for an account of how the conversion process works).

Easy as it certainly is to poke fun at certain of the more clumsily euphemistic terms, it is hard to use that clumsiness as a blanket reason for opposing inclusive language. Whatever the other arguments surrounding it, inclusive language is a civilizing factor in society simply by virtue of its very willingness to avoid giving offence once it has been made clear that offence is indeed given by the use of certain terms or descriptions. The danger in arguments over political correctness is always that in the rush to press the point about what may be seen as overly 'precious' avoidance of certain terms the participants lose sight of the main game, the fact that certain groups in society do in fact experience discrimination and that language is one of the prime determinants and/or mirrors of that discrimination. To focus merely on the language with complaints that so-called cosmetic use of language is an affront to the sensibilities of 'the ordinary citizen' and exhibits an overly sensitive, politically correct awareness of social niceties is to avoid this issue entirely. The term 'political correctness', Morris-Suzuki (1996) argues in an Australian context, is

> the intellectual equivalent of a Post-It: a neat little label which gives its users an illusion of having disposed of issues that they have not even begun to think about. Worse still, it is starting to smother any meaningful debate about appropriate ways of dealing with the real problems of prejudice, discrimination and social injustice which still clearly exist in our society.

'Kotobagari' arguments in Japan likewise privilege language over people, but fail to take into account the social repercussions of that stance. One of the social costs of continuing to use language and stereotypes known to be demeaning to certain sections of society is that members of those groups may be deterred from engaging in employment or other activities where they are likely to be targets, thus restricting their opportunities to participate fully in society. Another is that bad manners are allowed to reign: continued use in media reports of offensive terms without regard to the feelings of others openly reinforces a dominant ideology of homogeneity ('they're not like us') which excludes in discourse as it excludes in other areas where discrimination manifests itself, such as employment, marriage and education.

Political correctness causes anxiety through its challenge to what language should be, exposing the flaws in so-called 'common sense beliefs' about language (Cameron 1995: 120). Certainly the protests seen in Japan about 'kotobagari', like those about 'political correctness' in other countries, have focused on outrage at the idea that entrenched 'jōshiki' (common sense) in regard to certain terms should come under attack, no matter how often those of whom they are used explain that such terms embody discriminatory attitudes. Absent from the debate as carried out in Japanese newspapers and periodicals was any acknowledgment of the power relations codified in language; the staunchest defenders of the right to use whatever language they please saw the issue as one of cosmetic changes to 'accepted usage' rather than as involving a recognition of inequalities in society, which certainly would not be rectified by language change alone but where language change could provide one means of removing stigma. In other words, like opponents of political correctness elsewhere, they saw the 'ownership' of the language as under threat because of protests against its stigmatizing power from minorities; to allow substitutions for offensive terms would be to admit in the language to views other than those of the mainstream. In the Japanese case, this meant admitting to cracks in the ideologically sanctioned harmonious whole and to the presence of diversity in what was presented as a society without noticeable individual differences. The role of language in this view is not as a shaper of ideas but as a reflection of reality; for some, to be prevented from using terms which continued to express outmoded conceptions of social reality (particularly with regard to Burakumin and women) in deference to those who contested such representations was to admit against their will that the mainstream control of language was not value-free but reflected relations of power and domination inimical to the national myth.

In Japan, despite the longstanding national ideology of homogeneity and conformity, it may in the end be encroaching multiculturalism in the form of migrant workers and the increasing visibility of its own ethnic Korean and other minorities which brings about a change. Multicultural countries such as Australia where laws have been enacted to curb racial vilification argue that such legislation functions to educate an ethnically diverse society on the bounds of acceptable behaviour. Nobody would suggest that a law can put a stop to discrimination by changing people's thinking. It can, however, regulate behaviour on the street by imposing penalties for racist outbursts where a complaint is brought. In theory, the end result should be a society which is more aware of what its members have the right to expect in terms of behaviour – including language – from others and which areas are agreed to be no-go zones. As we saw in Chapter 1, the focus of what civil rights bodies exist in Japan is on education, without the backup of legislation except in cases where an offence against the criminal code is involved. It remains to be seen whether the increasing ethnic diversity experienced since the 1990s will prove to be the eventual catalyst for legislation.

## Literature and 'kotobagari'

The most vehement critics of 'kotabagari' have been writers, in particular those who argue that the use of discriminatory terms in historical fiction is merely a realistic depiction of how things were in the period being portrayed. Realism (or accuracy) is one of the most commonly heard defences of continuing to use contested language (Valentine 2002: 219), as is the appeal to constitutionally enshrined freedom of speech. It was the infringement of his right to freedom of speech that formed the bulk of Tsutsui Yasutaka's 1993 complaint. Some publishers (e.g. Kadokawa with Tsutsui) have defended their authors' right to use whatever language or stereotype they please. Many others have caved in to pressure to remove the words, fearing not only public embarrassment but also the effect adverse publicity might have on sales if they did not. Shogakukan, for instance, had to withdraw several thousand copies of its *Shinsen Kanwa Jiten* (a monolingual dictionary) in 1982 after a complaint from the Takatsuki Zainichi Chōsenjin Mukuge no Kai (Takatsuki Korean Residents Mukuge Society) about the inclusion of two discriminatory words, 'hokusen' and 'nansen', in an entry about the Korean War, and other protests have been carried out at the bookstores themselves (Yuasa 1994: 13, 16).

The Tsutsui incident led to an outbreak of debate on political correctness, with several magazines publishing special editions on the subject in early 1994. His experience raised questions as to what extent literary license should be permitted to override considerations of linguistic stereotyping. In March 1995, the Japan PEN Club surveyed 200 of its members to determine how valid were perceptions that there had been a marked increase in the policing of discriminatory expressions – symbolized by the 'iikaeshū' – since around 1970. The Club noted that these results were not representative of its very diverse membership as a whole: an earlier survey on discriminatory language in 1993 of its total membership of 1,606 had yielded replies from only 363, and the 200 to whom the 1995 survey was sent were drawn from this pool. Replies were received from 134 members. It is probably worth reproducing here the numerical statistics from the questionnaire, tedious though it may seem, in order to get an idea of the range of experiences and reactions.

Just under 80 per cent reported experiencing some form of editorial intervention requesting that they edit their writing to remove discriminatory expressions: 2.2 per cent indicated that such intervention occurred frequently, 42.6 per cent that it occurred occasionally, and 34.3 per cent that it occurred infrequently. When these three groups were further questioned as to when this had most often happened, 42.4 per cent reported that it had been more than ten years previously, 32.1 per cent that it had occurred between about 1986 and 1990, and 21.7 per cent from 1991 to 1995, indicating a decline in frequency. Most typical interventions had involved newspapers, magazines and books, with only around 10 per cent occurring during broadcasts, reflecting the respondents' main fields of activity. In the print media, which accounted for most of these, the most frequent incidents related to the categories of novels, non-fiction, plays and poems and to articles, essays and columns in magazines; in the spoken word, they related to expressions used in broadcasts and to a lesser extent in lectures and symposia.

Questioned as to the kind of expression which had provoked the intervention, just under half indicated that it had concerned discriminatory references to physical or mental characteristics, 39.8 per cent status and class appellations, 36.9 per cent race and ethnicity or region, 19.4 per cent occupation, 6.8 per cent gender and 1.9 per cent religious or political beliefs. In two-thirds of cases, the intervention had come from editors, directors or producers; in about a quarter it had come from people involved in groups working to eliminate discriminatory expressions. Other reported sources included administrators, event producers, readers/viewers and family/friends/colleagues. Reactions to the request had varied: 17.5 per cent had published the piece as it stood, refusing to accept any restriction on their freedom of expression; others (5.8 per cent) had published or broadcast it unchanged but appended an apology in a note or a brief announcement. On the other hand, some were willing to compromise: 65 per cent of respondents had substituted another word before publication, and 13.6 per cent had published with the offending passage deleted. A further 9.7 per cent had cancelled publication altogether.

Attitudes to the incidents also varied: while 9 per cent accepted that they had been wrong to use a discriminatory expression and 4 per cent believed they had been lax in editing, 35 per cent responded that it had been inevitable given the situation and 32 per cent registered disquiet, expressing themselves not convinced of the validity of the complaint. Twenty per cent gave other reactions which included things like deleting the expression in order to avoid embarrassing the publisher, and complying even though they had not meant any particular slight by the expression (Nihon PEN Kurabu 1995: 57–68).

Comments on the request for a rewrite ranged from the annoyed to the supportive and included remarks to the effect that rewriting simply cloaked discrimination, that language should be self-regulated and not regulated by others, and that the matter should be left to one's own good judgement. Some expressed support for the interventions, noting that objective education was needed to address the subjective issue of discrimination or that, since freedom and equality were basic human needs, authors should not use discriminatory terms at all. Others expressed concern about the classics: could classical opera still be performed if this sort of regulation increased? Chinese literature, it was pointed out, often contained references to physical attributes such as One-armed (person's name) or Limping (person's name), and these had to be translated. If there was no intent to discriminate, one respondent wrote, then it was impossible to discriminate no matter what one wrote (Nihon PEN Kurabu 1995: 80).

Literature, then, is considered a special case by many who produce it, and some argue that it should be exempt from restrictions on the type of language it can use. It has certainly featured prominently in the discriminatory language debate. Some complaints verge on the ridiculous: for example, the attack on the children's story *Momotarō* (*Peach Boy*) because of 'its description of *oni* (demons) as inherently evil creatures – a possible affront to people whose names contain the word *oni* – and for its use of the word 'retainers' to describe the dog, monkey, and pheasant that accompany the hero on his adventures' (Yoshida 1999).

Shimazaki Tōson's famous 1906 novel *Hakai* (*The Broken Commandment*), as was only to be expected, was an early target of the BLL. The book told the story of a teacher in rural Japan who struggled with the psychological consequences of having hidden his Burakumin origins from those around him. The first publication of this novel predated the 1922 formation of the Suiheisha (The Levellers' Society), the first national Burakumin group and the forerunner of today's BLL, which took as part of its manifesto a determination to 'thoroughly denounce' those who used words such as 'tokushu buraku'. Accordingly, *Hakai* became a focus for vehement discussion and objection to both the events of the plot and Tōson's own role in perpetuating what the Suiheisha viewed as discrimination against Burakumin by exposing them to public curiosity. *Hakai* was put on the agenda of the fifth national conference in 1926, with a view to determining whether a denunciation should be carried out against the author. In the event, the case for a denunciation was not upheld, even though the novel contained 71 instances of the word 'eta', 38 of 'shinheimin' and 6 of 'chōri' (all terms denoting outcast status). In 1929, however, after *Hakai* had been included in several major collections, Tōson voluntarily withdrew the novel from publication following an attempt by a breakaway Kantō Suiheisha group to extort money which led on to threats against his publisher, Shinchōsha. When the novel was once again published ten years later, in 1939, Tōson had removed all words such as 'eta', 'shinheimin', 'senmin', 'katō jinshu' (inferior race), 'chōri', 'yubi wo honhon' (four fingers) and 'yotsuashi' (four legs) and replaced them with 'buraku no mono', 'onaji mibun' (of the same status) and other similar neutral terms. In some cases the words were simply removed. The publisher approached the Suiheisha to work with them on this project (Andersson 2000: 149–61).

A report to the 1957 Buraku liberation national meeting made the BLL's position very clear: many literary works did no more than entrench existing stereotypes about Burakumin. No matter how good they might be perceived to be as literature, they could not be tolerated because they caused hurt. The Buraku liberation movement gave notice to those who 'lurked in the shadow of literature', creating poor quality discriminatory works, would find themselves squarely under attack, given the mass outreach of literature, film and stage plays (Buraku Kaihō Kenkyūjo 1980: 265–6).

It was not only literature containing reference to Burakumin that came under attack. In the 1990s, the word 'shina', meaning 'China' but carrying racist connotations from the way it had historically been used in Japan, was removed by the publishers from two literary works to be included in high-school readers and replaced with other less heavily freighted words. The first incident concerned the story *Kinosaki nite* (*At Cape Kinosaki*), written in 1917 by literary luminary Shiga Naoya (1883–1971). Hiroshima publishing firm Kyokasho Shuppansha, when it included the story in its *Revised Kokugo Ichi* (*Revised Japanese Language I*) reader, changed the phrase '. . . to iu shinajin' (a Chinese person called . . . ) to '. . . to iu chūgokujin' (same meaning) because of 'educational concerns'. A little later, when a piece from Nosaka Akiyuki's 1967 *Hotaru no Haka* (*Grave of the Fireflies*) was to be included in the reader *Kōkō Gendaibun* (*Modern Writing for High Schools*), the phrase 'shina ryōri' (Chinese cuisine) was replaced with 'chūka ryōri' (same meaning), apparently with the permission of the author. While the Ministry of Education, as it was then called, professed itself untroubled by the changes, Nosaka himself thought it would have been better educational practice to leave the word itself unchanged and append a note explaining its connotations or have teachers explain it in class. A journalist was quoted as saying that to change works of literature in this way (except in cases where the words concerned were clearly expressing discrimination against people with disabilities) was unacceptable, drawing as it did a veil over history. Students reading these books would never realize that once there had been a word 'shina' which had been used in discriminatory ways in Japan. Much better not to worry about using it but to explain the circumstances of its past (*Mainichi Shimbun* 1999). Apparently, people with disabilities should be spared the pain of reading past insults, but not those who had experienced racial discrimination, particularly those outside Japan.

The standoff continues between the two camps over whether literary works dealing with the past should be free to use terms which are avoided today but were common parlance during that period or whether words which offend modern sensibilities should be replaced with alternatives: 'There are of course no neutral un-constructed terms that avoid historical and cultural connotations' (Valentine 1997: 109, n. 8). It is those connotations which make the use of the words, even in their historical context, so unwelcome to those to whom they refer. But Kobayashi Yoshinori, a leading 'manga' artist, took aim at the Japanese refusal to discuss these issues openly when he published an attack on media self-regulation in his 1995 book *Declaration of Arrogance: Discriminatory Language Debated*, excoriating both the hidden discrimination still active in Japan and the silence surrounding it. Rather than ignoring discrimination by hiding particular language that encapsulates it, he argued, the important thing was to talk about it and attempt to arrive at a solution. Otherwise, no substantial change either in attitudes or conditions would occur.

## The internet

The 1990s saw not only the 'kotobagari' debate but also the emergence in the second half of the decade of a new arena for discriminatory language, the internet. For a time, after the media self-censorship lists kicked in during the 1980s, it might have seemed as though this policy had put a stop to the use of discriminatory language in public usage. The recent resurgence on the internet of expressions no longer found in the print and visual media and the efforts of Burakumin groups to combat this, however, indicate that far from being a dead issue, the struggle has merely shifted to a new arena. Moving on from the three phases mentioned by Yagi in Chapter 1, we have now entered a fourth phase in which online hate speech flourishes. It would be pleasing for the sake of symmetry to say that this fourth phase kept to the ten-year interval of the other three, first appearing in 2005, but in fact online hate speech was already evident by 1998. It deserves to be considered as a phase of its own, though, rather than an extension of the mid-1990s third phase, since the nature of the medium in which it occurs – if not the content of the expression – is so different from the earlier media interactions.

The advent of the internet has had both advantages and disadvantages for marginalized groups in Japan. Use of the internet has the potential to subvert the inability of such groups to be heard in mainstream media. This allows them to provide evidence refuting the hegemonic view of Japan as a harmonious homogenous whole. A BLL representative I interviewed in 1998 indicated that it was precisely the culture of silence about Burakumin in the mainstream media that he had sought to overcome by setting up a website where Burakumin could explain their own case; newspaper and TV stations would no longer allow that, for fear of subsequent reprisals. In the year since the site's establishment, he had had many hits, 80–90 per cent of which were from people with a genuine interest in addressing human rights issues, and the rest abusive. Even in the latter case, he had made email contact with the senders and had been able to convince some of them to change their misconceptions about Burakumin. Language self-regulation alone, he believed, would never bring about any real change in attitudes because it was done mechanically: words were substituted without any reflection on why the original words ought to be considered taboo. Personal contact through email, on the other hand, gave the opportunity to explain the realities of discrimination. In this sense, he perceived the internet as offering new opportunities.

On the other hand, despite the increased opportunity for exposure and contact among peer groups it affords, the internet's enabling conditions of anonymity and lack of borders have provided fertile ground for hate speech. In 2001, for example, 253 separate sites reviling Burakumin were discovered. In March that year, the BLL issued a proposal urging both the Japanese government and the United Nations to take action against discriminatory internet messages, which they broke down into three types: disclosure of the location of Buraku communities, allegations that certain celebrities were Burakumin or Koreans, and incitement to kill Burakumin (Buraku Liberation League 2001).

A particular focus for complaints has been the Channel 2 website (www.2ch.net/), which hosts unmoderated bulletin boards and list-serves on which discriminatory descriptions of Burakumin, people with disabilities, ethnic Koreans and many other groups frequently feature. Channel 2 was started in 1999 and has grown to be Japan's biggest collection of anonymous internet bulletin boards and discussion groups, covering a vast array of topics. It has at times attracted censure for its role in several notorious incidents, such as allowing the real name of a boy accused of killing a child to be published there. Users occasionally take advantage of the different readings available to kanji to reproduce taboo words using kanji phonetically, for example, the word 'shine!' (die!) can be written with the correct kanji as 死ね、or with 師ネ、氏ね.[1] Threads dealing with people with disabilities frequently contain words like 'korose!' (kill them) or exhortations to kill and eat babies with disabilities; others dealing with Burakumin sometimes contain postings simply repeating the words 'eta, hinin!', 'BURAKU-KICHIGAI' (Buraku = crazy) and 'baka Buraku' (stupid Buraku).[2]

It is again the BLL which has been at the forefront of moves to ban racial and other types of discriminatory messages and sites on the internet. Associated groups have been set up specifically to monitor this issue. In 1999, an article in the *Buraku Liberation News* noted an increase in the following types of discriminatory postings and activities during that year:

• messages posted by students;
• copying and reproduction of web pages which had been banned from other internet service providers (ISPs);
• use of offshore servers rather than servers in Japan;
• providers who ignored complaints about discriminatory postings;
• number of neo-Nazi xenophobic websites (Tabata 2001: 7).

Hate groups have a tendency to use ISPs in countries other than the one to which their remarks are targeted, and this has been the case in Japan too. In August 2000, a statement on discrimination on the internet to the United Nations Subcommission on the Promotion and Protection of Human Rights called on the United Nations High Commissioner for Human Rights to begin information-gathering on good codes of conduct by ISPs and on any legal measures in force to prevent such use of the internet. This stance was backed up by the Japan Bar Association in 2001 when it made a statement to the World Conference against Racism to be held in South Africa that year, calling in part on United Nations member states to draft an action plan for regulation of expressions intended to promote racial discrimination on the internet.

The small but active Network against Discrimination and for Research on Human Rights (NDRH, Hansabetsu Nettowaaku Jinken Kenkyūkai)[3] was formed in May 1997 following a report to a BLL branch of a website for the Society to Protect the Yamato Race, which advocated the preservation of Yamato (or mainstream) Japanese values and consisted of 15,000 postings slandering *inter alia* people with disabilities and Burakumin. Upon receipt of complaints from the BLL, which had been informed of the site by several sources, Niftyserve, the ISP, deleted the site 'based on its bylaws'. Following this incident, an initial NDRH group consisting of eight members, with Tabata Shigeshi as its one-person secretariat, was formed the following month and immediately lodged a complaint with certain racially discriminatory bulletin boards on Niftyserve's Bulletin Board Corner. Over the following years this small group expanded their activities and opened their own bulletin board and homepage on Niftyserve (http://homepage2.nifty.com/jinkenken/).

The NDRH functions by having its members (who can be anyone in any country with an interest in human rights) report to it incidents of online anti-Burakumin and other postings. In 2000, it reported nearly 70 complaints about websites containing incitements to racism, which it broke down into eight main categories as follows:

1 Defamatory to particular individuals.
2 Misconceptions about Burakumin and their environment.
3 Voicing prejudice learned from relatives.
4 Criticisms of the liberation movement, especially of the BLL.
5 Graffiti-type postings which just parrot statements like 'exterminate the eta!' over and over.
6 Racial/ethnic postings induced by reports in the mass media, for example, criticism of ethnic Koreans every time the news reports a North Korean missile suspicion.
7 What the report calls 'pedants showing off their knowledge' by making general (but erroneous) claims about Burakumin.
8 Other types: if someone causes trouble in some way, and it is reported in the papers or on TV, it will often be said in internet postings that the person must be Burakumin or ethnic Korean.

A much smaller organization with links to the NDRH is INDI, the International Network against Discrimination on the Internet (Intaanetto-jō no Sabetsu ni Hantai suru Kokusai Nettowaaku).[4] The INDI website is actually not maintained by any formally incorporated organization but is the result of the personal efforts of Nakahara Mika in tandem with the NDRH's Tabata Shigeshi. The home page defines INDI's mission as lobbying for international action against cyberdiscrimination, in the belief that action within national borders is ineffective given the global reach of the technology and that ISPs tend to be reactive rather than proactive in their handling of the issue. The INDI home page stresses the belief that no real discussion has ever resulted from the posting of discriminatory messages on websites or bulletin boards: providers have either overlooked such postings or have immediately deleted the messages, but without having any clear policy on guidelines for the future. The matter should not be left in the hands of individual governments, therefore, but should be tackled 'internationally, by nongovernmental organizations (NGOs), via the Internet'. NGOs and individuals are more likely to be successful in uncovering infractions than any government body could be, and should work in tandem with the authorities to stamp them out. In a recent email, the site owner commented that 'INDI may not be as active as it should and want to be; however, it is still alive and hopes that it will take a more active role to fight against cyberdiscrimination'.

A further organization set up in late 2000 is the New Media Human Rights Organization.[5] This group runs 'Furatto', a home page[6] dedicated to providing up-to-date information on human rights via the internet. The aim of the website, writes chairman Mushakoji Kinhide, is to provide an electronic space for the frank discussion of a range of important human rights issues and to give heart to those experiencing discrimination, with the long-term aim of changing attitudes in the community (Mushakoji 2002). The Furatto site offers online rights-related information in 11 categories, including issues relating to Burakumin, people with disabilities, women, ethnicity, sexuality, children, health and ageing. For each category it offers a bulletin board where people affected by discrimination can discuss their experiences, and an 'Ask an Expert' service. It has 21 affiliated groups, among them universities, government bodies in the Osaka region, Burakumin groups, welfare groups and other human rights groups. Mushakoji is affiliated with Osaka's Asia Pacific Human Rights Information Centre. The Buraku Liberation and Human Rights Research Institute also maintains a study group on discrimination on the internet, as do several other organizations.

To give just a very small example of the kinds of language-related education carried on by NDRH: on its Suiheisen bulletin board, we find a discussion of whether the term 'buraku' itself can be considered discriminatory or not.[7] Saya, living in the Tōhoku region of north-eastern Japan, had emailed to say that in that area's dialect villages were customarily called 'buraku' but that she had learned at school that this word was considered 'sabetsu yōgo' in the Kansai area: was that in fact the case? Responses from others varied. The NDRH's Tabata replied with a long message explaining that the word 'buraku' itself was not discriminatory: if it were, the teacher would have been very much in error in teaching it to students. As the dictionary shows, the word simply means 'a small hamlet' and was used in certain village contexts. Despite this, the word had come to be used with discriminatory overtones in prefectures which had Burakumin hamlets, but it all depended on context and intent: the Suihensen bulletin board site itself, for example, used the word in discussions of how to solve Buraku issues, and that was certainly not discriminatory. The term 'buraku' only becomes a problem when used in phrases such as 'Aitsu wa buraku no mon dakara' (that's because he's from the buraku) or 'Buraku no yatsura wa kowai yatsura ga ōi' (lots of those buraku guys are scary) – i.e. when it is used as a put-down, in which case it is not the word itself that is discriminatory but the intent with which it is used. He reassures

Saya that the dialect use of 'buraku' in Tōhoku she has described is not discriminatory, backed up by the fact of his own Burakumin background.

'Ksuke' (Keisuke) from Kansai, however, assured Saya that in his part of Japan the word 'buraku' was recognized as being discriminatory and that she would be well-advised not to use words likely to be offensive to others; it seemed the further north one went in Japan the lower was likely to be the awareness of human rights issues. Anyone living in Tokyo should be careful what they said, since people came from all over Japan to the capital.

This drew a second response from Tabata, who agreed with 'Ksuke' that to say 'anata wa buraku' in Kansai could be very offensive, but stuck by his argument that language could not be considered in isolation from intent. This was just as true of language relating to people with disabilities as it was of language relating to Burakumin. It was true that, as Saya had said, the word in her area was part of the local culture; one just had to be careful to ensure that it was not linked on that account with any overtly discriminatory intent in using it, and one should put oneself in the shoes of those to whom such language was commonly addressed with abusive intent in the Kansai area and ponder the issue.

Kō chimed in with a recollection of the time when the administration in a town in Yamagata prefecture several years back had suggested that they abandon the use of the term 'buraku' to mean 'village' in publicity for a national athletics meet for fear that people would think there were Burakumin living there, an event which Tabata remembered with disgust.

Discussions about language similar to the above not infrequently figure on the bulletin boards. Taken all together, these initiatives add up to a determined presence on the web aimed at fighting cyber-discrimination and giving those who have experienced discrimination a forum to discuss what has happened to them and to seek advice and information. The notion of agency is very important; even if their voice is as yet small, and these sites are run by a very few people, they are active in making their voice heard.

In the general internet domain, 'kotobagari' is a favourite topic for discussion on chat groups across a wide spectrum of internet users. A recent Google search on the term turned up 13,300 hits. A dominant theme in postings is the strongly expressed belief that media self-censorship is undertaken not out of any real concern for human rights or injury to the feelings of others (despite the cover statements) but out of fear of public embarrassment following complaints, especially since the complaint may not come in the form of discussion but of threats, demands for money, violence and tactics such as the 'endless fax'. Everybody, it seems, has a story to tell or an opinion to express on the topic, such as that it is easier to tinker with the language which serves as a code for underlying discrimination than to address the real issue of discrimination itself. Cynicism and irreverence are the usual hallmarks of the dialogue, regardless of the position espoused. People often comment that media replacement of problematic words is not done with any real consideration of the issues involved but rather involves an automatic, mechanical substitution of sanitized terms for others whether or not they are used in a context with obvious intent to demean.

A search of Japanese search engines using the terms 'sabetsugo', 'sabetsu yōgo' or 'sabetsu hyōgen' turns up frequent links to discussion groups where these issues are debated, sometimes heatedly. A website at http://members.jcom.home.ne.jp/ksmiracle/Kokugo/Taboo.html lists multiple links to online dictionaries of 'sabetsugo' or 'hōsō kinshigo' (words not to be broadcast), and has links to Google searches on the words 'sabetsugo', 'sabetsu yōgo' and 'hōsō kinshiyōgo' which in turn spawn multiple further links to pages on these topics. Some of the sites are long-established, others transitory, but the level of interest is high and the internet allows interaction between people who might not otherwise have a chance to discuss these issues.

## Dictionaries

Some adjustment to dictionary entries has occurred in many countries as a result of increased sensitivity to stereotyping. A South African dictionary of Afrikaans, for example, operates on a policy of omitting many racist terms in common use. The director of the Australian National Dictionary Centre, interviewed in 1995, noted that dictionary editors 'are becoming more fearful of the influence of powerful pressure groups and recent government legislation such as the 1994 Racial Vilification Act' (Hill 1995). Burchfield (1989: 111) also refers to the pressure brought to bear on dictionary editors by pressure groups keen to see certain unpleasant terms deleted from the wordlist.

This harks back to the old argument over prescriptivism versus descriptivism and poses a challenge to the supremacy of the descriptivist position in lexicography. In Australia, the third edition of *The Macquarie Dictionary* (1997) adopts a compromise position, including words which may be considered 'offensive, derogatory or taboo' but placing a warning next to them. Others, however, take a harder line, arguing that the language merely reflects society and should not be changed until society itself changes:

> The ultimate solution to the problem of appropriate ter-minology and nomenclature does not lie in the censorship of dictionaries on whatever grounds, but, rather, in a broader social amelioration of prejudice and discrimination against those who are different from ruling power groups whether because of their skin color, sex, sexuality, national origin, ethnicity, religious beliefs, political convictions, or bodily condition. When the social problems which spawn such linguistic correctives disappear, it will no longer be neces-sary to change the language.
>
> (Boletta 1992)

The connection between naming and reality is thus disregarded. But as Benson (2001: 4), discussing centre-periphery metaphors in the *Oxford English Dictionary*, reminds us, 'the modern dictionary is . . . not simply a book about words, but also a book about the world viewed through the particular window of the word. Ethno-centrism in the dictionary thus becomes a question both of the presentation of the language and of the representation of the world as it is inscribed within the structured version of the language that the dictionary presents to the user'. Taking issue with the underlying assumption of the dominant descriptivist paradigm that descrip-tions of language are objective, Benson argues quite rightly that dictionaries are representations rather than transparent descriptions of language and that they represent 'a historically situated form of discourse' (p. 23). That being the case, the omission from recent Japanese dictionaries of some of the words contested, particularly those relating to Burakumin, indicates a decision to ignore rather than acknowledge the contested status of certain words, i.e. the same attitude of 'putting a lid on a stink' found in the press.

A quick search for a few contentious terms on an online Japanese dictionary (http://dictionary.goo.ne.jp, accessed 2 September 2004) which searches four Sanseido dictionaries turned up one hit for 'bikko' (cripple) in a monolingual Japanese dictionary and one in a bilingual Japanese-English dictionary. 'Eta' did not appear in the bilingual dictionary but was explained in the monolingual *Daijirin* as a class discriminated against both in the pre-modern and modern periods and given the characters meaning 'great filth' 'in a spirit of discrimination'. That particular entry was followed by a link to the entries for 'Buraku Kaihō Dōmei' (BLL) and 'hinin' (non-person). Interestingly, despite the link to the Buraku Kaihō Dōmei entry in the *Daijirin*, the word 'Burakumin' itself is not listed; nor does it appear in the bilingual dictionary. The online *Sanseido Web Dictionary* at www.sanseido.net/ returns a hit for 'eta' in the monolingual *Deiri Konsaisu Kokugo Jiten*, defining the word as a status discriminated against in the Edo Period (1603–1867) and marking it as 'sabetsugo'. It does not appear in the bilingual Japanese-English dictionary.

The 1954 third edition of Kenkyusha's *New Japanese-English Dictionary* defines the word 'eta' as 'the *eta* caste; a pariah; a social outcast', with none of the sociological explanation of the Sanseido *Daijirin*, and marks it as V (for vulgarism: 'unpleasant words which do not form part of the usage of ordinary people'). The categories of labelling do not include 'sabetsugo'; despite the activism of Buraku support groups since the 1920, 'eta' in this 1950s dictionary was marked only as something polite society did not mention, rather than as a word judged to be discriminatory. The word is not included at all in the 2003 fifth edition of the dictionary. Likewise missing is 'tokushu buraku', which appears in the 1954 edition defined as 'an outcast ( = untouchable) community'. 'Burakumin' is not mentioned, but 'Buraku Kai' is given as 'the National League of the Outcast Communities'. In the 2003 edition, 'Buraku Kaihō Domei' is given as 'Buraku Liberation League', the official name of that group. 'Hisabetsu Burakumin', the term preferred by the BLL until 1997 when it substituted 'buraku jūmin' (hamlet residents) for 'Burakumin', appears in neither. In fact, no term relating to the Burakumin can be found in the dictionary, resulting in their lexical invisibility. With regard to disability, 'bikko', 'mekura', 'tsunbo' and 'kichigai' all appear without annotation. Words which have been the focus of protest by the women's movement, such as 'shujin' (husband) and 'kanai' (wife), are included without any notation to indicate that some consider them derogatory.

Table 2.1 lists some of the words that have been identified as problematic by Burakumin, people with disabilities and women's groups and their occurrence in two editions of Kenkyusha's *New Japanese-English Dictionary*. This shows the power of the BLL to bring about through threat of public humiliation the erasure of references to its members so that those words no longer figure in the latest editions of certain dictionaries. The fact that words found

*Table 2.1* Problematic words

| Word | 1954 third edition | 2003 fifth edition | Marked? |
|---|---|---|---|
| eta | √ | X | V |
| tokushu buraku | √ | X | No |
| burakumin | X | X | |
| shujin | √ | √ | No |
| kanai | √ | √ | No |
| bikko | √ | √ | No |
| mekura | √ | √ | No |
| tsunbo | √ | √ | No |
| kichigai | √ | √ | No |

problematic by other groups still appear with no marking to indicate this supports the view that articulate disputation of semantic issues is not enough to change entrenched social views, even to the point of indicating by a dictionary tag that those words are disputed. It requires organized action and public protest to bring about such change, and that is what has happened in the case of the Burakumin.

For example: the 1969 second edition of the *Kōjien*, a monolingual dictionary first published in 1955, was deliberately revised by its publishers, Iwanami, following an incident in which they were targeted for denunciation by the BLL after a article in their journal *Sekai* included the words 'tokushu buraku'. The first edition had defined the word 'buraku' as 1) a hamlet, and 2) an abbreviation for 'tokushu buraku'. In the second edition, the first definition remained the same but the second was expanded to explain that the word indicated a place where people lived who had experienced severe status and social discrimination, created in the Edo Period; even though status distinctions had been abolished by law in the early Meiji Period, social discrimination had not yet disappeared. Appended was the term preferred by the BLL, 'mikaihō buraku' (unliberated villages) (Yōgo to Sabetsu o kangaeru Shinpojiumu Jikkō Iinkai 1989: 33), followed by 'tokushu buraku'.

The same second edition *Kōjien* defines 'eta' largely in terms of occupation and feudal status, at some length: 'an Edo Period class relegated, with the hinin (non-persons), to below samurai, farmers, artisans and merchants and in receipt of no taxes or tributes. They lived in specified areas and engaged mainly in working with hides, as well as making bamboo tea whisks, lamp wicks and sandals. The term was abolished in 1871 and they became citizens'. The word 'eta' is given only in hiragana and is marked as a linguistic corruption of 'etori', elsewhere defined as 'people who make their living by slaughtering animals, tanning leather, selling meat and making feed for falcons and hunting dogs'.

Although this seems a very careful definition, the BLL did not approve of such occupation- and origin-based descriptions on the grounds that they did not sufficiently take into account historical research on Burakumin origins and thus perpetuated occupation-based discrimination. Unlike other books, they argued, dictionaries, once bought, are subject to repeated use. Because users have confidence in the authority of their definitions, it is very important that dictionaries impart a proper understanding through accurate description of matters relating to Burakumin and take care that definitions do not become outdated. Dictionaries had been a problem for Burakumin since the time of the Suiheisha, but by 1988, the BLL thought, they were beginning to show signs of improvement (Buraku Kaihō Dōmei Chūō Honbu 1988: 112–3).

In 1984, publisher Sanseido revised around 30 definitions relating to women and elderly people in the *Shin Meikai Kokugo Jiten*, a monolingual dictionary (Takagi 1999: 143). Almost ten years later, however, problems remained with sexist dictionary definitions. Endō (1993: 397–8) surveyed 30 editions of small-format dictionaries for their definitions of the word 'onnadatera', in which the suffix 'datera' (unsuitable for/unbecoming to) is added to the word for 'woman' to mean 'unfeminine/unwomanly'. She found that 23 dictionaries had entries for both 'onnadatera' and 'datera'; in the latter case, 'onna' was given as the example for 'datera'. In view of the fact that the social role of women has greatly changed since the eleventh century in which this term originated, 'by continuing to use "onnadatera" as the predominant example for the suffix -datera, dictionaries reflect society's prejudice and reinforce dated stereotypes of women'. Her aim is not to have such words and phrases, of which she offers several other examples, removed from the dictionary, since they are aspects of historical fact. Rather, dictionaries should warn users of the derogatory connotations and the historical background, since users view the dictionary as authoritative and therefore such discriminatory expressions are perpetuated 'as if they were the norms of Japanese usage'.

In terms of disability, in 1991 the National Association for People with Intellectual Disabilities (renamed Inclusion Japan in 1995) requested publisher Heibonsha to revise the definitions given in its *Tetsugaku Jiten* (*Dictionary of Philosophy*) of 'seishin hakujaku' (intellectual disability, lit: feeble-minded) on the basis that they could give rise to discrimination. The publisher complied, got rid of the stock in the warehouses, recalled those copies already distributed to bookstores and inserted an amendment (Takagi 1999: 121–2). A recent (2003) informal survey of ten monolingual dictionaries, all published since 1995, found that the words 'kichigai', 'tsunbo', 'bikko', 'mekurameppō' and 'mōmoku' (blind) appeared in all of them, but that six had tagged at least one of those terms as discriminatory. Two dictionaries, the 2002 *Meikyō Kokugo Jiten* and the 2000 *Deirii Konsaisu Kokugo Jiten*, marked all five as discriminatory (Gally 2003).

Having regard to the notion that context of use is all-important, Landau (1984: 188) says of the basis on which judgements of 'derogatory' status are made:

> The decision to label a word offensive is rarely based on reasoned discussion of what one or a group of people have actually experienced. It is based on the editor's judgment of society's norm for the limits of reputable public behaviour . . . Labeling of insult, then, is essentially political and moral. The lexicographer is taking a stand on the side of those who deplore racial and ethnic bigotry. He is also deflecting criticism for including offensive terms by showing his repugnance for them.

Such labelling, Benson (2001: 47) agrees, represents a judgement that words so labelled are outside the social norm, and it is this that Endō wants to see in the case of terms such as 'onnadatera'. Clearly, in more recent dictionaries, certain of the words relating to disability also fit this description. The *Kōjien*, however, still tags only one word as discriminatory: 'tokushu buraku' (Gally 2003).

It was to the dictionary and its tags that Tokyo governor Ishihara Shintarō turned in April 2000 to defend his use of the term 'sangokujin' (third-country people), considered highly discriminatory by Japan's resident Korean population. The incident concerned, which will be discussed in greater detail in Chapter 4, involved Ishihara's use of this term in a speech to the self-defence forces linking 'sangokujin' with the rise in crime in Tokyo and resulted in a storm of protest from ethnic Korean groups and others. In the days that followed, Ishihara continued to maintain that he had not meant the term to be discriminatory and had not in fact realized that it was, invoking the dictionary where it was marked as 'zokushō' (colloquial) and not 'besshō' (derogatory) as his legitimizing authority.

This incident encapsulates the confusion many feel about the nature of language deemed discriminatory: if it is not marked as such in the dictionary (and it usually is not), then it cannot actually be discriminatory, an attitude which ignores the decades of emotional baggage a word can build up through use in discriminatory contexts, to the point where the word itself becomes anathema to those it stigmatizes. There is thus a good case for dictionaries to ensure that they are sufficiently familiar with social issues involved in this sort of linguistic transaction to enable them not to delete but to mark as 'derogatory' those words likely to offend on racial, ethnic or other grounds.

We have examined in this chapter three different aspects arising from the discriminatory language debate: the political correctness backlash, the rise of the internet as a forum for language use denied in other media, and the changes wrought in dictionaries as a result of activism. We now move on to an examination of the activities of the groups involved in protesting linguistic stereotyping, beginning with the first and most vocal of all, the BLL.

# 3

# STATUS DISCRIMINATION

Of all groups which have protested against language demeaning to their members, the most active and successful – if we take 'successful' to mean effective in preventing recurrences – has been the BLL (Buraku Kaihō Dōmei). Indeed, Burakumin support and experience have contributed to campaigns for recognition of the rights of other groups in the postwar period. The BLL includes other human rights issues in its brief in addition to those solely Burakumin-related and has been vocal in its support of other minority groups. Its publications comment on issues of concern to other groups (see Tomonaga 2002b, for example, for a BLL protest against threats and harassment of Koreans living in Japan in the wake of the 2002 return of Japanese citizens abducted by North Korea) and take part in their meetings (e.g. see *Kaihō Shimbun* 2002 for a report of a women activists' conference). This stems not only from concern with the general human rights situation in Japan but also from the fact that Burakumin are themselves likely to be members of other minority groups: Burakumin women, for example, or Burakumin with disabilities. Many ethnic Korean residents live in Buraku areas where they are accepted as fellow victims of discrimination (Fukuoka and Tsujiyama 1992) as do people with disabilities. The BLL has received messages of appreciation from Ainu groups and from South African black groups, announcing their intention to emulate the BLL (personal interview with BLL member 1998).

The roots of this influence, of course, lie in the earlier start to Burakumin campaigns. The first national Burakumin organization, the Suiheisha (Levellers Society), formed in 1922, was already conducting denunciation campaigns in the 1920s, whereas for groups such as people with disabilities, women and ethnic Koreans it took postwar international movements in addition to domestic conditions to provide the enabling conditions for protest, or at least for that protest to be heard. The Ainu people were marginalized in the geographical sense up in Hokkaido as well as in the political and economic senses, and as well as being fairly strongly assimiliated were too reduced in numbers to form groups with any chance of making a difference. The Utari Kyōkai (Ainu Association of Hokkaido) was not formed until 1946 and was assimilationist in orientation. By the time these groups began their postwar consolidation, the BLL already had several decades of experience which were often deployed to the benefit of others.

Before I begin to talk about the language issues the Burakumin have contested, a brief discussion of this group, who experience ongoing status discrimination, is in order. Who are the Burakumin and why do they fight discrimination? Why are these people, biologically indistinguishable from other Japanese and yet ostracized and marginalized since the mediaeval period, so important – almost the lynchpin, we might say – for any discussion of language and discrimination in Japan? The Burakumin are Japan's largest minority group, thought to number around 3 million. As with any status-determined minority, exact numbers are difficult to pinpoint – government figures give a much lower estimate (1.2 million in a 1993 survey) but take in only those listed in official Buraku areas, while Burakumin activist groups point to the fact that many of their number choose to live outside such areas. The actual figure, the Buraku Liberation and Human Rights Research Institute suggests on its website (http://www.blhrri.org/), is closer to 3 million, living in 6,000 Buraku communities.

Neither race nor language marks Burakumin as in any way different from other Japanese; they are themselves Japanese, physically indistinguishable from the rest of the population, and hence have been called 'Japan's invisible minority' (Wetherall and de Vos 1975). This has not stopped mainstream Japanese society from suggesting a difference in racial origins, however: Burakumin are rumoured to be descendants of Koreans taken prisoner and brought to Japan 1,500 years or more ago. No reliable evidence supports these ethnocentric claims, which seek to consign uncomfortable facets of Japanese society to the comfortable dustbin of 'not really us at all': conversely, they also reveal 'a way of thinking that condemns a person to near subhuman status if he/she is not Japanese' (Hane 1982: 139).

Burakumin suffer from ongoing status discrimination stemming from the fact that in feudal Japan their families were outcasts, not even registered on the four-tier class system (warrior/farmer/artisan/merchant in descending order) because of their involvement in lowly and undesirable occupations. These usually, although not always, had to do with polluting activities such as those associated with meatworks, tanneries, cemeteries and garbage removal: occupations which contravened both Shinto and Buddhist strictures on pollution, 'kegare', an important ongoing theme in Japanese society. During the Tokugawa Period (1603–1867) Burakumin were referred to by the term 'eta', now considered highly derogatory; as we saw in Chapter 1, the two characters used to write this word mean 'highly polluted' or 'great filth'. Membership of this group was hereditary. Other occupations included making bamboo, dyed and metal goods, guarding fields, labouring in temples and working in transport. In addition, an associated group known as 'hinin' (non-persons) worked as travelling entertainers, beggars and executioners (Sugimoto 2003: 174). 'Hinin' status, unlike that of 'eta', was not passed down through the generations. This word, perhaps more than any other, encapsulates the ethos: putting somebody outside society dehumanizes them, and to be explicitly referred to as a 'non-person' rams that home.

During the premodern period the ancestors of many of today's Burakumin were ostracized and forced to live in hamlets separate from the mainstream communities, often on land that nobody else wanted, for example, in river beds. The modern term 'Burakumin' thus means 'people of the hamlet', referring to these special places, segregated from the mainstream villages and towns, in which Burakumin were required to live in order to keep their polluting presence away from other Japanese. The first volume of novelist Sumii Sue's multi-volume *The River with no Bridge* (1961–73) provides a compelling fictional account of life in such a village in the early years of the twentieth century, where the river divides the Burakumin village from the mainstream village: while residents crossed the actual bridge spanning the river every day, in fact it is the symbolic river dividing the two communities which cannot be bridged. Such settlements were often excluded from maps, and their residents were counted with the suffix for animals (-hiki) rather than people (-nin). A famous 1859 court judgement ruled an 'eta' to be worth only one-seventh of an ordinary person, so that anyone who killed one 'eta' would need to kill another six before he could be brought to justice (Passin 1955: 255). Not fully human; not remotely to be considered on the same legal footing as their fellow Japanese. Activities which denoted a common humanity, such as eating, drinking or smoking with or near other Japanese, were strictly prohibited.

Enforced segregation, together with a set of strict rules of conduct imposed with the aim of preventing normal social intercourse with mainstream Japanese, led to a continuing status discrimination which is far from extinct today. Following the Meiji Restoration, the former four-tier class system was replaced with a two-layer system of aristocrats and commoners/citizens ('heimin') and an Emancipation Edict (1871) freed the former 'eta' from their lowly (or non-existent) status. What this meant in practice for the Burakumin, however, was that many lost out in economic terms. Whereas former samurai were compensated, outcasts lost their economic monopoly over certain occupations and many found themselves in even more reduced circumstances than before. Others who suffered economic hardship at the same time came to live in Buraku areas, with the result that not everyone who lives in those areas today can trace their ancestry to those who were formerly designated 'eta' or 'hinin'. A second wave of economically distressed people moved into the Buraku after World War II. The general populace does not discriminate between residents of these areas, however: 'not any kind of continuous descent but the mere fact of being born into or living in certain residential areas – the Buraku – exposes this section of the population to discrimination' (Kaneko 1981: 119).

Living conditions in many Burakumin areas have improved as a result of twentieth-century activism and government policies. In 1969, following the establishment by the prime minister in 1965 of a Dōwa[1] Policy Council, a Special Measures Law for Dōwa Projects was enacted with the aim of improving living conditions in designated Buraku areas and improving educational participation rates through special scholarship funds. Those settlements which received aid under the policy were designated 'dōwa chiku'. Under this legislation, the national government provided two-thirds of the cost of Dōwa Policy activities undertaken by local governments. Two other related laws, the Special Measures Law for Regional Improvement Projects (1982) and the Special Measures Law Concerning the National Budget for Specified Regional Improvement Projects (1987), further contributed to the improvement in living conditions thus brought about.

Not all Burakumin areas have benefited, however: a 1987 government survey found that only 4,603 of the total 6,000 buraku had been designated as 'dōwa chiku', so that more than 1,000 had not received the benefits offered by the policy, and living conditions there remain poor. Upon expiration of the Special Measures Law in 2002, 'Burakumin relief funds' were cut by more than half, and the number of special projects reduced from 1,700 to 1,000, in recognition that the Burakumin living standards the Law had originally been set up to improve had in fact improved as a result of special funding (US Department of State 2004). The BLL continues to call for comprehensive surveys (the first since 1993) to determine whether or not the cessation of the special measures is appropriate or whether new measures ought to be put in place.

Despite these material improvements, however, the social stigma of coming from a 'dōwa chiku' remains strong. People known (or even suspected) to be from such backgrounds can find marriage partners harder to find. The same is true of employment, although steps have been taken to ease this by no longer requiring applicants to give full details of where they were born. Because Burakumin look just like other Japanese, the only real clue to their status is to be found in the place where they live. Even this is not always reliable, given that, as we have seen, many residents of designated Burakumin areas are not themselves descendants of premodern outcasts but economically disadvantaged mainstream Japanese. Some people with disabilities, or Koreans, or others, have also moved into the 'dōwa chiku' to take advantage of the government subsidies available there (see Fowler 2000: 19, re. Koreans). Reber (1999: 300) offers the following inclusive definition of Burakumin: 'those people who were born, brought up and living in *buraku*, those who were not from *Burakumin* family but came to live in *buraku* in the recent past and those who are living outside the *buraku* but have blood relationship with *Burakumin* – all these are considered the *Burakumin* minority by the majority Japanese'.

The belief that place of origin or residence is a sure indicator of outcast descent remains strong, however, and has resulted in several blacklist scandals. In the 1970s, employers, including large companies, were found to be buying lists ('chimei sōkan') giving details of areas Burakumin were likely to come from (for details, see Buraku Liberation League 2002a).[2] During subsequent investigations, the *Buraku Liberation News* (2002b) reported:

> it was disclosed that 'Buraku Lists' were traded as a 'counter-measure' to the rising trend of Buraku liberation movement that brought about the unified job-application form for high school students and the restriction of the perusal of family registers . . . By looking into the motives of the companies which bought 'Buraku Lists', it was also disclosed that discriminatory practices in employment had been shrewdly done, in addition to obtaining the 'Buraku List'; they recruited students only from designated schools, and used the applicant form made by themselves that have

discriminatory questionnaires and tried to know the personal background of the applicants as much as possible through interviews and examinations.

While there is no national law – the BLL's preference – outlawing the use of these lists, in 1985 Osaka Prefecture enacted an ordinance regulating investigation of personal backgrounds of a type designed to 'out' Burakumin, followed by Kumamoto, Fukuoka, Kagawa and Tokushima Prefectures. As we saw in Chapter 1, the BLL has always argued in favour of national-level legal sanctions designed to prevent discrimination, a route the Japanese government has been reluctant to follow. The local regulations, however, have not been sufficient to stop the practice: in 1998, it was discovered that at least 400 companies had requested an investigative agency to investigate the personal details of job applicants, including whether or not the applicants were from Buraku areas (Tomonaga 2001). This case is still under investigation. 'Chimei sōkan' have also been discovered circulating on the internet in the last couple of years. Most bulletin board requests for information about areas where Burakumin come from relate to the Kantō area around Tokyo; in Osaka – where Burakumin have historically been more heavily concentrated – the areas are more likely to be known already.

The fact that family registers were until 1976 open to perusal by anyone interested played an important role in contributing to anti-Burakumin discrimination, particularly in the matter of the blacklists described above. Registers contained information on where the family's main residence was; if traced far enough back, to the first appearance of family registers in 1872, the presence of the terms 'shin' (new) in front of the designation 'heimin' (commoner) or 'moto eta' (former eta), used after the 1871 Emancipation Edict for Burakumin to designate families of such status, clearly indicated to those who wanted to know that the family in question was a Burakumin family. Despite the government's insistence that the registry is value-neutral,

the family registry cannot be value-neutral because value judgments adhere to the required information in ways that create and maintain hierarchies of worthiness and participation in Japanese society. Individuals are excluded, or restricted in participation, on the basis of others' knowledge of negatively valued elements of their family registries.

(Bryant 1991: 112)

The BLL (1998: 2–8) reproduced a collection of actual examples of personal history documents submitted with job applications which had been annotated by investigators. The symbol ✳ near someone's address meant that the address had been identified as being a Buraku; the numeral 4 inside a circle on the paper meant that the person was of Burakumin descent, as did a circled letter D (for Dōwa). Once the symbol ✳ was noted, no further investigation as to the suitability of the applicant for employment was conducted; they were automatically excluded.

Given this degree of continuing social prejudice, mention of the Burakumin remains by and large an unspoken taboo in polite Japanese society, despite the introduction of elective Dōwa educational programmes in approximately half Japan's 47 prefectures and the establishment of Chairs of Dōwa Education in around 40 per cent of Japan's universities and colleges (Buraku Liberation League 2002e). It is not unusual to find Japanese who profess never to have heard of Burakumin. The silence extends to the highest levels: the United Nations rapporteur who commented on the Japanese government's first and second periodic reports to UNCERD in 2001 noted that the report was silent on important issues such as that of the Burakumin. Referring to the discrimination experienced by Burakumin, the rapporteur concluded: 'Surprisingly, the authorities had not mentioned their plight, which was well documented both abroad and in Japan' (CERD 2001: 29). Reference to Burakumin is often erased from Japanese translations of western books, or attempts are made to do so: the Japanese translation of Michael Crichton's *Rising Sun* is one example, as is Karel van Wolferen's 1989 *The Enigma of Japanese Power* (see Wetherall 1992a). Also in the 1990s, a short story containing reference to Burakumin was omitted from the Japanese-language edition of *Encounters with Japan*, a collection of essays and works of fiction by Australians familiar with Japan (Taylor 1997: 39).

One reason often given for the lack of domestic discussion is the paucity of press coverage of Burakumin issues, which as we have seen in earlier chapters stems from past experience with protests over unfavourable reporting. Journalist William Wetherall (1992b) has disputed this, pointing out that in 1992 a woman's magazine was running a series of articles about a case of ancestry-related marriage discrimination, that another women's magazine had published a five-page article on Burakumin issues and an apology as the outcome of a BLL denunciation against it; and that both TV Asahi and NHK had featured programmes on Buraku discrimination.

In two of these cases, the information was published/broadcast in response to denunciations carried out against the magazine and TV Asahi respectively; in other words, it was published under duress. An American reporter working for NHK was surprised to be told, when he suggested a story about Burakumin and the leather market, that 'the story was too sensitive . . . the government did not recognize minority groups in Japan, and furthermore . . . to call attention to minority groups would only make their situation worse' (Sherman 1994). Online searches of newspaper archives have not produced many instances of reporting of Burakumin issues in the major dailies, apart from an occasional mention of the BLL's political activities or articles on museums or historical sidelines. Where articles do mention Burakumin, as in the case of a report in the *Kobe Shimbun* on 13 May 1998 referring to the setting up of a human rights website, they invariably use the term 'hisabetsu buraku' to refer to Buraku areas.

If the topic of Burakumin should happen to arise in conversation, voices will often be lowered, or perhaps a certain discreet display of four fingers will be made. Four fingers are held up to indicate that Burakumin work with dead animals (e.g. as butchers or tanners), or are considered to be like animals themselves. The word 'shi' (four) is especially freighted with meaning here because it is a homonym for death in Japanese. Where mention is unavoidable, the issue is usually spoken of as the 'buraku mondai' (Buraku problem). The words 'neta ko o okasanai' (don't wake a sleeping baby) may be murmured: don't talk about it – if nobody actually knows about Burakumin, they will not speak badly of them or discriminate against them.

This phrase has often in the past been invoked by Burakumin themselves, those unwilling to stir up the discriminatory backlash which many have found follows action (see e.g. Hane 1982: 255). It is not a position espoused by the BLL, which argues that active discrimination against Burakumin is in fact occurring, particularly with regard to employment and marriage, and that people do know, often from their earliest years, of the existence of Burakumin:

> It is important, therefore, for everybody to be correctly taught about the Buraku problem without having the reality covered over. If we leave 'a sleeping baby' as he/she is, prejudice and false understanding will be taught for generations and Buraku discrimination will be continuously reproduced.
>
> (Buraku Liberation League 2002d)

## Burakumin and language

As a result of this entrenched social ostracism, the Burakumin have been particularly vulnerable to both outright unpleasant description and linguistic stereotyping. The use of the term 'eta', introduced in Chapter 1, has been likened to that of the hostile 'nigger' in the USA (Brameld 1968: 106; Neary 1989: 11). In her *A River with no Bridge*, author Sumii Sue vividly portrays the anguish felt by Burakumin children at primary school in the early years of the twentieth century when this term is thrown scornfully at them by other children.[3] Following the formation in 1922 of the Suiheisha, Burakumin began to take concerted action against insulting language. In order to target organizations and individuals who engaged in discriminatory behaviour, both actual and verbal, the Society developed a strategy known as 'kyūdan' (denunciation), which during the 1920s and 1930s 'was a form of organized protest which was as specific to the *Suiheisha* as the withdrawal of labour of the industrial union or the refusal to pay rent of the tenants' union . . . *Kyūdan* was not just the only *Suiheisha* activity that most *burakumin* took part in but was also the only manifestation of the movement's activity that the majority population encountered' (Neary 1989: 85).

The first campaigns in 1922 involved protests about the words 'eta', 'doetta' and 'yottsu' (meaning 'four', and accompanied by the derisive holding up of four fingers referred to above).[4] Complaints were made to the user and usually an apology settled the matter, although sometimes a public retraction in print was demanded in more severe cases. Some incidents involved police action where violence resulted from a refusal to apologize. The number of such campaigns peaked at 1,462 in 1923–4, but continued at the rate of around 500 or so per year, sometimes more, until well into the late 1930s (Neary 1989: 111, 134). This period saw the beginning of censure of newspapers which carried articles using discriminatory language in reference to Burakumin, marking the first instances of what would grow into the postwar campaigns described below.

Following a period of wartime suppression, the Suiheisha was replaced in 1946 with the National Committee for Buraku Liberation, which in turn became today's BLL. The strategy of denunciation continued: a report to the 1951 national meeting noted that incidents of discrimination had latterly been particularly frequent and discussed the role of journalism and its attendant social influence in this. The three major newspapers – the *Asahi*, the *Mainichi* and the *Yomiuri* – with their combined circulation of many millions, had run discriminatory articles about Burakumin in June, July and August that year; several magazines, including the influential *Bungei Shunju*, had done the same, thereby continuing to entrench the divide between Burakumin and other Japanese by confirming mainstream attitudes of superiority (Buraku Kaihō Kenkyūjo 1980: 69). Fowler (2000: 24) notes that an incident in that same year (1951) in which the BLL denounced the city of Kyoto, the employer of a public servant who wrote a derogatory story about Burakumin entitled 'Tokushu Buraku', rather than the author himself 'inaugurated . . . what was to become the *buraku* community's new strategy of focusing denunciations nationwide not on individuals but on institutions, with the intent of influencing policy'.

It was through the frequent use of denunciation by the BLL in the postwar period that the battle against discriminatory language in public discourse was brought to the stage where media organizations, fearing the public embarrassment such confrontations involved, began the policy of self-censorship described in Chapter 1. We have seen that while this outcome was undoubtedly favourable in the BLL's eyes, it also contributed to the culture of silence surrounding the Burakumin in society at large. On the other hand, though, if the manner in which discussion was to be carried on involved the use of terms unacceptable to those to whom they referred, then better silence than insult. Since the special measures adopted by the government had gone a long way to improving conditions in Buraku areas, discrimination had now become more and more a cultural (rather than economic) problem: thanks to the widespread reach of the mass media, discriminatory ideas could now be widely circulated and it was therefore seen as all the more important that media organizations police their use of language (Shiomi and Komatsu 1996: 225–6).

The BLL maintains the strategy of denunciation today, believing it to be – in the absence of any laws protecting people against discriminatory personal attacks – the best way of ensuring that such attacks do not go unpunished. In its view, the measures laid down by the Ministry of Justice's Civil Liberties Bureau for dealing with such cases – namely, seeking to educate the offenders about the civil rights of others – are insufficient and do not have the power to prevent recurrences: 'Although the constitution advocates the protection of human rights, the law and the system leave discriminatory acts to take care of themselves. In short, were it not for the Buraku liberation movement, people of Burakumin backgrounds would just have to accept discrimination meekly' (Buraku Liberation League

2002c). Denunciation has in the past been judged a legally legitimate tactic by the Japanese courts (Taylor 1997: 40).

Denunciation, the BLL advises,

> allows Buraku people to accuse persons who discriminate against them. It seeks to have them reflect and apologize. Through this process, both the discriminating person and Buraku people discover the background in society which produces discrimination. The ultimate aim of denunciation is to educate the person who was discriminated against, to help probe why discrimination still exists and to awaken the dignity of humanity.
>
> Such protests need to be organized (rather than individual) actions because incidents of this kind anger the entire Buraku community; because group action gives strength to the weak; because group action is more likely to get results than individual protest, as experience since the formation of the Suiheisha has shown; because prejudice is a widespread social problem and not just an individual problem; and because the presence of the group acts as a brake on the potential for unruly individual responses.
>
> The history of the Liberation Movement is also the history of denunciation: the Movement has made a big progress through denunciation. It discouraged deep-rooted discrimination in society, including any carried out in the name of the law . . . Without denunciation, discrimination could have become rampant. Various circles including education, mass media, corporations, and religious group could not have noticed Buraku discrimination.
>
> (Buraku Liberation League 2002c)

In the case of the 'chimei sōkan' incident referred to above, denunciation appeared to have had favourable results at first:

> Being strongly denounced, the companies which bought the lists have repented. Companies, such as based in Tokyo and Osaka, have formed federations to commit themselves to eliminating Buraku discrimination. Since 1977, by the instruction of the Ministry of Labour, companies with more than one hundred employees have to assign a staff member to promote Dowa education as an in-house training.
>
> (Buraku Liberation League 2002b)

Nevertheless, this was not sufficient to root out the practice, as the 1998 recurrence shows, although in that case the investigative agencies involved voluntarily reported their discriminatory inquiries to the BLL Osaka (Buraku Liberation League 2002b).

On one occasion in the 1990s, denunciation was used as a kind of proxy weapon by a Keio University student who sent postcards to members of the BLL in Tokyo claiming to have discovered that they were Burakumin and that their secret would be exposed unless they paid 5 million yen each. The postcards purported to come from the principal of the junior high school attended by the student and from his classmates there. When the truth was eventually discovered (for details, see Buraku Liberation and Human Rights Research Institute 2000), the student (who was subsequently expelled from the university) announced that in using the names of those who had bullied him at school and of the principal who had not intervened, he had hoped that the BLL would 'deputize the revenge' on his behalf, through their well-known tactics of inquiry and denunciation.

For many years, the annual report to the BLL's national conference had listed in its section relating to the struggle for development in relation to cultural activities the same phrase: 'we will deepen people's understanding in regard to discrimination and language, and will fight against instances of discrimination in publishing and the mass media'. In 1995, however, a little more was added:

'In cooperation with the denunciation struggle headquarters, we will wrestle with instances of discrimination in publishing and the mass media. In relation to issues of language and discrimination and so forth, this financial year we will actively establish a forum for wide discussion. We will also deepen our links with the Sabetsu to tatakau Bunka Kaigi and the Jinken o kangaeru Bunka Kankeisha no Kai'.

(Uesugi 1995: 90)

This increase in attention to the topic was no doubt prompted by discussion following on from the wave of public debate in 1994 about political correctness and 'kotobagari' which followed the Tsutsui Yasutaka incident, as described in Chapter 2.

In the case of the 'chimei sōkan', then, denunciation brought about the enactment of local regulations designed to put an end to the problem, but such regulations proved insufficient in the long term to prevent recurrences. In the case of language use, however, much more lasting effects have been achieved, although as we have seen not without vigorous criticism from certain sectors of society. Takagi (1999: 31) lists three main categories of terms which have drawn protests and in some cases full-scale denunciations: historical terms of contempt such as 'eta' and 'hinin'; the allegorical use of words to indicate inferiority or ostracism, as in the 'tokushu buraku' (special village) cases discussed below; and expressions relating in general to social status, parentage/family and lineage. Further examples of the first of these are 'chōri' (which relates to the crime-related jobs today done by the police but formerly done by Burakumin, including the detention and surveillance of prisoners, executions, searching for criminals and so on), 'saimin' (paupers), 'kyōmin' (the indigent), 'chōrippo' and 'chōrinbō' (in parts of Kanto and Kyushu), 'kawata/kawatanbō' (Kansai area); 'hachiya' (Shimane area) and many more. A term particular to Edo (Tokyo) was Danzaemon, originally the name of the seventeenth-century head of the Iyano family who lived in Asakusa and controlled the 'eta/hinin' groups in the city and the surrounding Kanto area but used by extension to refer to Burakumin (Takagi 1999: 34). So controversial are these old terms that the website of the Osaka Human Rights Museum[5] feels it necessary to preface its contents with the disclaimer that it uses the terms 'eta', 'kawata', 'hinin', 'tokushu buraku' (and others relating to Koreans and Ainu people) only as historical terms meant to highlight the discrimination faced in past eras when those terms were in common use.

'Shinheimin' is a particularly sensitive historical term, denoting as we saw the determination to continue social ostracism despite official changes to social structure. Markers of difference were meant to linger. Not only did the presence of this term on a family register clearly indicate that the family were formerly 'eta' or 'hinin', even the posthumous Buddhist names given by temples to Burakumin have been found to identify them as such after death (Bodiford 1996: 7).[6] The repercussions of the terminology changes of the emancipation edict were that 'shinheimin' and 'suiheimin' 'came to take on the full insulting overtones of the term "eta" they replaced' (Passin 1955: 249). What Passin termed this 'problem in terminological etiquette' had been resolved, he thought at the time of writing, 'in favour of the term "tokushu buraku", which means "special community", so that it is customary to refer to them today as Burakumin, or people of the community'. Time was to prove him wrong on this point, however; the term 'tokushu buraku' in media reporting was to prove incendiary to the BLL and has been one of the most contested terms of the whole debate over language. A series of incidents in the 1950s and 1960s involving the major newspaper *Asahi Shimbun* and resulting in protests from the BLL illustrates this. Most involved the use of 'tokushu buraku' to refer allegorically to some sort of unacceptable behaviour or social ostracism on some particular group's part.

The term 'buraku' itself, as we have seen, refers to a hamlet or village, or the people who live there. As such it is unproblematic, and takes on overtones of being associated with 'undesirable elements' only when it is prefixed by 'tokushu' or 'hisabetsu' (discriminated-against villages, a term created by the BLL in the postwar period).[7] The term 'tokushu buraku' was created by the Meiji government to refer to the villages where outcasts lived. 'Special' here functioned to segregate. Although it was taken out of official documents from the beginning of the Taisho Period (1911–25), it remained in general use as a synonym for such villages and also as a way of indicating inferiority or worthlessness. Indeed, it figures today on the BLL's web page, where the top page explains: 'the term "tokushu buraku" has been figuratively used from time to time in distinguishing a different society from a so-called ordinary society as well as in describing Buraku areas, resulting in fostering discrimination against Buraku people' (Buraku Liberation League 2002d). Although the term was used by Burakumin themselves in the declaration which founded the Suiheisha in 1922, which called upon 'tokushu Burakumin' throughout the country to unite, the BLL notes that it was used by those whom it designated in a spirit of defiance in that instance; it was thus a matter of those demeaned reappropriating the term used to demean them. In no other circumstances is it acceptable, and its use has been vigorously pursued.

In a column about the arts in the *Asahi* of 1 January 1956, for example, literary circles were described as displaying a 'tokushu buraku-teki' narrowmindedness ('the sort of narrowmindedness one finds in a tokushu buraku'). The manner in which this incident was handled became the model for later censure of the media by the BLL (Takagi 1999: 35–6). The League lodged a complaint with the *Asahi*'s Osaka office and received an apology from the editor-in-chief, who admitted that the paper had been careless in using the expression and would be more careful in future. This did not satisfy the League, however; they announced that what they wanted was not an apology alone but the kind of reporting which would contribute to eradicating discrimination. A special unit dealing with the selection of material on Burakumin topics was thus set up in the 'social issues' section of the Osaka office and seven articles were featured in December that year.

Ross (1981: 202, 203), in a paper dealing primarily with sexist and racist terms in the United States, argues that 'metaphors . . . are our primary vehicles for conveying attitudes'. Even though, in the Japanese case, 'tokushu buraku' has been argued by non-Burakumin to be a dead metaphor (one which has become detached from its origins and passed into standard usage), 'the implications of dead metaphors are known or accessible to their speakers, while etymological details often are not', and it is those implications which are important. While a young Japanese person today might not consciously be aware of the historical origins of the term 'tokushu buraku', the fact that it has been customarily used to compare other referents with something undesirable weights the metaphor with a prejudicial implication.

To digress for a moment: the term 'hisabetsu buraku' (discriminated-against villages), preferred by the BLL because it highlights the proactive stance of the mainstream in perpetuating discrimination, may not be that much better and may in fact be counter-productive. Overt statements of victim status such as this often result in the opposite of the effect desired, pushing those who might originally have been sympathetic into adopting a defensive stance which leads to a discounting, if not an outright denial, of the original claims. The self-image being fostered by this term is consonant with the strategy favoured by the BLL, but is likely to produce no more than a yawn from many. As Marks (1999: 140) notes, 'it is important to look not just at the manifest meaning of a statement, but also to examine how it functions for the self-image the speaker is attempting to project'. Fowler (2000: 2, n. 4), in reference to this term, adds that 'this usage is not without negative ramifications: it underscores the difference between marginalized communities and majority society while suppressing differences *between* various *buraku*'.

Returning to my main point: the 'tokushu buraku' term was used in *Asahi* publications or by *Asahi* employees on a total of seven occasions during the 1950s and 1960s, including the one just described. Fed up with this, the central headquarters of the BLL announced a full-scale denunciation of the company in November 1967. In the accompanying documentation, the League made the point that no matter how pure the intentions of the writers or how socially affirmative the text surrounding the words 'tokushu buraku' might be, the persistent use of the term itself in their view contributed to increasing and perpetuating discrimination against Burakumin; it was on that account that the denunciation both of the writers themselves and of the *Asahi* as a company was made. They did not accept the argument that the terms were used 'unconsciously' and that nothing derogatory was meant by them; this 'unconscious use' concealed ongoing attitudes of anti-Burakumin discrimination and perpetuated stereotypes (Takagi 1999: 35–9).

It was at this point that the League's attitude toward discriminatory language in public discourse, always stern since the 1920s Levellers days, hardened into the unyielding stance which was to bring media organizations to heel. While some might see this as attacking the symptom rather than the cause, the League's policy was that this particular symptom actually facilitated the cause in an ongoing vicious circle, and that the best way to get to the underlying deeply buried roots of discrimination was to discourage the use of the language which it spawned. Whether or not this policy has been successful in terms of its ultimate aim is a moot point; the recent rise of anti-Burakumin attacks on the internet in Japan would suggest that it has not. Nevertheless, that was the trajectory on which the League fixed its sights, with significant consequences for Japan's editors. Language in this view played a 'lighthouse' role: where certain words and phrases occurred, the rocks of discrimination could not be far away. Language is not seen in any way as constructing reality but as an instrument to be used against people, like any other weapon; it is the reality of discrimination which gives birth to the language. This stand on language involves confirmation of control over identity and also incorporates the BLL's sense of moral responsiblity and community obligation, given the support they have on occasion given to other groups protesting linguistic stereotyping. Through the uncompromising fight-back strategy of denunciation, they reject the identities others assign them.

The *Asahi* was not the only target of attack over the use of the 'tokushu buraku' term. Over the years, a host of other incidents where it was used drew censure from the League, ranging from newspaper and magazine articles and references in books to television programmes, political press releases and even a 1982 lecture at a school Parents and Teachers Association meeting. One of the best-known is probably the article published in the magazine *Sekai* in March 1969 by a Tokyo University professor, in which he used the expression 'daigaku to iu tokushu buraku' (the special enclave that is a university). The process was as follows. A complaint was issued by the League. The magazine's publishers, Iwanami Shoten, then recalled the issue and put out a revised version. The next issue in April contained an insertion slip explaining that the publishers had taken this unprecedented step of recalling the March issue in order not to contribute to the perpetuation of discrimination through editing slips on the company's part; they unreservedly apologized for the mistake. The May issue then carried an article by the offending author in which he too apologized and criticized his own innocent but thoughtless use of the term: he had meant to imply that Tokyo University was a national institution which monopolized aristocratic privilege in the world of scholarship and that this privilege should stop (see Takagi 1999: 39–43 and also Yōgo to Sabetsu o kangaeru Shinpojiumu Jikkō Iinkai 1989: 32–3).

In 1982 a Justice Bureau Director remarked at a research symposium on implementation of duties that 'the rather unsavory parallel has been drawn . . . that public servants are as much a fact of life as the *tokushu buraku*. But public servants are after all, just human beings'. Commenting on this incident, Hirasawa (1991: 200–1) notes three ways in which these words are problematic: a senior government official seemed unaware of how derogatory this term was considered, despite a 1965 government report admitting the discrimination Burakumin continued to face in postwar Japan; the human/non-human contrast of public servants and Burakumin; and the lack of protest from the audience, also high-ranking officials.

Tactics employed in the denunciation campaigns were not always peaceful. In 1973 the League launched a succession of complaints against the media, centring mainly on Osaka and North Kyushu, in which the scale and method of the denunciation involved was much greater than before. Common to all the complaints was the use of semi-violent threats and unusual intimidation over the use of words. Media managers and individuals who were approached in these incidents are reluctant to speak of what happened, but they appear to have been approached by groups styling themselves 'kakuninkai' (confirmation tribunals) who asked whether they thought certain words they had used were discriminatory or not. If they agreed that they were and apologized, they were then asked whether they thought an apology was sufficient, and the threats continued until further redress was promised. If they maintained that their words were *not* discriminatory, they were subjected to several hours of grilling until they accepted that they were at fault. These complaints were put into action by large groups of League members (Yōgo to Sabetsu o kangaeru Shinpojiumu Jikkō Iinkai 1989: 8–9), earning it a reputation for harassment which still features in the public mind today.

An example of this sort of campaign is the case of Terebi Nishi Nihon (TV West Japan) in northern Kyushu. In April 1973, this station broadcast as its late night movie the 1959 Daiei film *Ukigusa* (*The Floating Weed*), in which the hero is a wandering performer whose son wants to marry a woman in the troupe but is advised not to as he and she are 'jinshu ga chigau' (of different races). The local branch of the BLL took great exception to the reference to 'travelling player' (a traditionally Burakumin or hinin occupation) and 'of different race', arguing that the film went against the spirit of the government's 1969 Law on Special Measures for Dōwa projects which made funding available to improve conditions for Burakumin. The initial response from the channel was to argue that the film should be taken on its merits as a whole and that as it was an artistic work from an earlier time, complaint on the grounds of discrimination was inappropriate. To this the League replied that such an answer indicated complete ignorance of the nature of discrimination. Members lodged complaints with everyone from the company president down, until finally, after an all-night meeting, the channel capitulated. Five promises were extracted: that a letter of apology would be issued, a 30-second television apology would be broadcast, the company would carry out research on Burakumin issues for an hour a week and would broadcast a programme twice a month aimed at enlightening viewers on these issues, and finally that the company would participate in study and training meetings run by the League.

The TV apology (Owabi Supotto), which was broadcast for a week, ran as follows: 'on 17 April last we broadcast the Daiei film *Ukigusa* late at night. The theme of discrimination on the grounds of occupation runs through the film as a whole, and in it the chief of the travelling troupe says to an actress that his son and she are of different races (jinshu ga chigau), which ignores basic human rights and was inappropriate to the broadcast. We sincerely apologize for having broadcast this film'. Two programmes dealing with the League, one of them – *Ningen* (*Human Beings*) – 30 minutes long, were made. The final demand, however, that of in-house study and training meetings was not met to the satisfaction of the League: the company's labour union, believing that the meetings to be an intellectual attack on the union, boycotted them, so that although Friday-afternoon meetings were held within the company, only those with non-union jobs attended (Yōgo to Sabetsu o kangaeru Shinpojiumu Jikkō Iinkai 1989: 10–11).

This incident typifies what became the pattern for BLL denunciations in North Kyushu. Such tactics became common during the

1970s and 1980s, and explain why the media were so anxious to avoid becoming a target. Not all media outlets did this, however: while the major ones drew up lists, smaller companies did not, so that even as late as 1989 complaints were still being made about the use of words such as 'eta hinin'. In that year, for example, the magazine *Computer Access*, distributed to subscribers by mail, carried a description of people unfamiliar with laptops and personal computers as being like the 'eta hinin' of their day.

The four-finger gesture attracted attention on several occasions. In 1973, it had been removed from an advertisement for Ripobitan D which said 'ヨツ！お疲れさん！' (loosely translated as 'calling everyone who's tired!'). The ヨツ (yo followed by a half-size tsu) was clearly intended as an exclamation to get people's attention and would not have been pronounced 'yottsu', which would have been written with a yo followed by a normal-size tsu. Nevertheless, when it appeared in the newspapers, it was changed to 'ヨオ！' (yo-o) to avoid any possible resemblance to the Burakumin-related derogatory term. In 1974 a revised version of an elementary school arithmetic textbook was issued; it had formerly featured drawings of hands holding up the relevant number of fingers in relation to the numbers 1 to 5, but because one of these was of a hand with four fingers held up, the drawings were dropped from the revised version (Yōgo to Sabetsu o kangaeru Shinpojiumu Jikkō Iinkai 1989: 59–60, 100). In 1983, a panellist on a Nihon Terebi (Japan Television) broadcast made this gesture when referring to 'yakuza' (gangsters), implying a connection between Burakumin and organized crime. Sensitivity to the significance of the gesture occasionally led to over-reaction: on the same programme's 'Best Five of Everything' segment, the order had been shown by holding up the relevant number of fingers, but this practice was discontinued for fear that it would cause misunderstanding in the case of the number four.

A further source of friction during the 1980s was the use of the expression 'shi-nō-kō-shō [something]' to indicate that whatever word occupied the [something] position was at the bottom of the status ladder, as when, for example, the *Asahi* carried an article describing tour conductors as 'mibun seido de iu to, shi-nō-kō-shō no shita ni tsuakon' ('in terms of social status, tour conductors are lower than everyone else'). (Takagi 1999: 70). This is an example of Takagi's third category of terms inflammatory to the BLL, those involving reference to social status. The problem stems in this instance from the fact that in feudal times the official class system, as mentioned earlier, ranked people into the four classes of 'shi (samurai)-no (farmer)-kō (artisan)-shō (merchant)' – what followed this, never mentioned in the official ranking, was 'eta/hinin'. To continue to use this term even metaphorically was in the League's view to perpetuate status discrimination.

The 'eta' word still crops up now and then, mostly in semi-literate graffiti ('kill the eta!') and on the internet. Many of these incidents are reported in the BLL's publications. To list just a few examples: the headquarters of the Buraku Liberation Research and Education Centre in Osaka were twice sprayed with the words 'etta' and 'die, etta' in early 1998 (Buraku Liberation and Human Rights Research Institute 1998), while in May 2002 the words 'eta wa kitanai' (eta are filthy) were discovered on a public toilet wall in Tosashimizu City (Buraku Liberation and Human Rights Research Institute 2002a). In November 2002, the *Kaihō Shimbun* reported that a student at Shikoku Gakuin University had several months earlier been sent mail containing the message 'shine eta 4 burakumin meiwaku da' (die, eta! 4, burakumin are trouble) (Buraku Liberation and Human Rights Research Institute 2002b). Neither of these latter incidents was allowed to pass unchecked. In each case the BLL held public meetings attended by city and schools officials (in the Tosashimizu case) and with university staff (in the Shikoku Gakuin case) to discuss the incidents and make clear their opposition to attacks of this sort. A list of further such incidents, sufficient to give an indication of the type of message sent, can be found in Section 7 of Tomonaga (1998). Incidents of this sort, impossible to police, nevertheless are not allowed to pass unchecked by the BLL when reported. Responses from the authorities rarely lead to prosecution, although in 1997 a man was sentenced to a year in prison for defacing public facilities with anti-Burakumin graffiti (Buraku Liberation and Human Rights Research Institute 1997).

## Differing viewpoints

The above discussion has centred on the language-related activities of the BLL, but there are in fact other Burakumin groups, most prominent among them the Zenkairen (an abbreviation for Zenkoku Buraku Kaihō Undō Rengōkai, the National Buraku Liberation Federation) which split from the BLL in 1976 over political differences and adopts a very different view of both the denunciation tactic and of the efficacy of protesting against language use. The basic point of disagreement between the BLL and the Zenkairen, which is supported by the Japan Communist Party (JCP), lies in the manner in which discrimination is to be tackled. Whereas the BLL pursues a policy of direct confrontation of specifically anti-Burakumin discrimination from a human rights perspective, the Zenkairen favours the line of a wider and more inclusive proletariat class struggle approach which includes all oppressed groups, not just the Burakumin, in its ambit. The Zenkairen was particularly opposed to the special measures adopted by the government to improve conditions in designated buraku, believing rather in integration rather than separatism in the struggle for economic justice. With regard to language, the Zenkairen believes the denunciation approach is more likely to be counter-productive than to lead to any real social integration in the long run; hate speech and discriminatory graffiti should be ignored rather than attacked. Of these two major groups, it is the BLL which is the major focus of Burakumin activities *vis-à-vis* government, media and the wider community.

In 1976, the BLL published a lengthy tract explaining its views on how to deal with discriminatory language in order to counter what it called misconceptions perpetuated by distorted reporting on the matter in the JCP's *Akahata* (*Red Flag*) newspaper. The Miyamoto faction of the JCP had gone on the attack against the BLL's denunciation tactics, describing them to the general public (or at least, to those of the general public who read *Akahata*) as anathema to freedom of speech and aimed at instilling a culture of fear among writers, editors and artists. The BLL hit back with an argument that their denunciations were not meant to censor but to persuade; democracy itself was being questioned in postwar Japan, and the JCP would do better not to make the language issue a political football but to rethink both the discriminatory structures entrenched in language and the meaning of democracy itself. For the Miyamoto group to label denunciations as violence, as it had, was to regenerate the discriminatory attitudes of the general populace. Contrary to the JCP claims about the creation of 'iikaeshū' sections pertaining to people with disabilities and other non-Burakumin groups, the BLL stressed that it had never undertaken an actual denunciation over discriminatory language which did not relate to Burakumin, and that denunciations could not therefore be blamed for any language change which related to other groups. The BLL itself in principle opposed the idea of lists of taboo words, which merely displaced the problem on to the words alone and did nothing to address the underlying discrimination. Media organizations were not creating them because they had been moved by persuasion, but because the management had told them to do it, in the manner of 'putting a lid on a stink'. The claims by the Miyamoto faction that protests against 'tokushu buraku', which after all only meant 'special village', should be discontinued were summarily dismissed: the BLL did not know of one single case where the term, used as a simile, was not pejorative. Places described as some sort of 'tokushu buraku' were invariably ugly, backward, unclean or had a bad image. The whole point of denunciation, from which they would never resile as a tactic, was to be progressive by awakening public awareness of discrimination, not repressive by restricting freedoms. Denunciations, it was stressed, were never carried out just because a particular word had been used but only after the BLL had looked at the whole context of its use and determined that it had been used with intent to discriminate (Buraku Kaihō Dōmei Chūō Honbu Shikikyoku 1976).

The standoff between the Zenkairen and the BLL continues, with the former remaining resolutely opposed to the latter's denunciation tactic and taking pains to make it known to the international (i.e. English-speaking) community. The homepage of the Arai branch of the Zenkairen[8] restricts itself to Japanese in all but one clearly strategically-targeted English-language document. This document, meant for United Nations perusal, accuses the BLL and its IMADR offshoot[9] of brutal violations of human rights: 'we have decided to publish this . . . to provide accurate information for U.N. bodies and member countries on the violent activities of the Buraku Liberation League, the core body of IMADR, with accurate information on human rights issues in Japan'. The reference to violent activities means denunciations.

In 1992 a new group, the Buraku Kaihō Dōmei Zenkoku Rengōkai (National Federation of Buraku Liberation Alliances), or Zenkokuren, was formed as a 'new people's organization of Burakumin to fight against Buraku discrimination' in place of the BLL. Zenkokuren's website (www.zenkokuren.org) explains in highly emotive language that the formation of the group was motivated by several factors: the collapse of the bubble economy and the subsequent economic downturn; the government's embarking on a new 'war of invasion' by sending troops to Cambodia and the Middle East, and its plan to cease Dōwa funding measures; and above all, a 1989 Ministry of Justice document advising against participation in denunciations. The BLL, it was argued, had lost its focus on still existing discrimination and become indistinguishable from the Zenkairen. Zenkokuren, therefore, harking back to the original Suiheisha declaration that 'the time has come when we can take pride in being eta', took as its platform a militant activism with a particular focus on renewed denunciation as the means of achieving improvements in Burakumin lifestyle and a determination to carry on working-class resistance to imperialist wars at grassroots level.

One example of this activity in relation to the internet occurred when, taking exception to anti-Burakumin threads on Channel 2 message boards, Zenkokuren announced a strong denunciation of the website, not only on the grounds of the distress and suffering caused to the targets of the vituperation but also on the grounds that many of the attacks were made under the banner of 'freedom of speech'. Unlike the BLL stance, where what was sought was the removal of such messages from the sites concerned, the Zenkokuren approach was that (in cases of possibly unconscious discrimination stemming from ignorance of the facts) continuing publication of messages casting slurs on Burakumin should be allowed in order that they could be rationally refuted through public debate with Zenkokuren members and the posters: in other words, a proactive rather than reactive process, like that of the early Suiheisha which Zenkokuren took as its model. Posters of outright hate speech messages such as 'die, Burakumin!', however, should be afforded no mercy and made to take responsibility for their actions (Zenkokuren n.d.).

As we saw in Chapter 2, the rise of internet technology has seen a revival of the kind of anti-Burakumin language formerly used in the print and visual media, free from the media self-censorship imposed there. The anonymity of the internet has provided fertile ground for those who wish to avoid the constraints of other media. The NDRH (Hansabetsu Nettowaaku Jinken Kenkyūkai),[10] as we saw, was set up following discovery of one particularly virulent website which advocated the preservation of Yamato (or mainstream) Japanese values. The owner lamented what he argued was an increase in people with disabilities and hereditary diseases; criticized Burakumin denunciations and what he saw as the BLL's 'victim mentality', and regretted the fact that government money had been unfairly diverted from mainstream Japanese into the Dōwa projects. The purpose of his organization was to counter this situation so that the Yamato bloodline would not be extinguished. This kind of electronic vilification has meant that the BLL has had to find new tactics, and that is why the small but active online anti-discrimination networks described in Chapter 2 have been formed.

With the use of discriminatory language in the media effectively under control and attempts being made to assert some measure of control over language on the internet, the one remaining area of concern is the enactment of a racial discrimination law which would outlaw vilification.

Concerned that the Special Measures Law would leave many issues unsettled when it expired in 2002, a group was set up well ahead of time in 1985 to draft a Fundamental Law for Buraku Liberation, which was to have two main thrusts. The first was to ensure the continuation of active government intervention to improve Buraku living conditions and participation rates in education and employment. The second was to create a discrimination-free society through a systematic programme of public education on human rights issues and a government crackdown on discrimination in employment or other areas, to be accompanied by the establishment of a human rights committee (for a discussion of the BLL position on this law, and the Zenkairen opposition to it, see Reber 1999).

In 1996, some years after this campaign began, the government enacted the Law of Promotion of Measures for Human Rights Protection. This law, effective for five years, stipulated that:

> the government is to take the responsibility of promoting measures concerning education and inculcation to enhance the level of understanding on the concept of respecting human rights among citizens; and aid for the victims in cases of infringements on human rights. It also determines ... to establish the Council for Human Rights Promotion, which consists of up to 20 of the commissioners to examine and review the basic matters regarding the above measures.
>
> (Ministry of Justice 2002)

The BLL at the time welcomed this move as an interim step towards its desired Fundamental Law for Buraku Liberation (Buraku Liberation League 2002d), but it was not long before dissatisfaction set in. In 1997, the first meeting of the Council for Human Rights Promotion was held after its 20 members were selected from a diverse range of backgrounds. However, the BLL was not happy with the lineup (which did not include people with active experience of discrimination) or with the fact that the meetings were not open to the public (although the minutes were made publicly available). It proposed an alternative council whose members had first-hand experience of discrimination (Tomonaga 1997). When the Bill was taken up again in 2002, the BLL issued a statement detailing the flaws in the previous version and the committee working towards the Fundamental Law for Buraku Liberation also mobilized its members to appeal.

The five major flaws found with the proposed revision were set out as follows: the Human Rights Commission would be an organ of the Ministry of Justice and therefore not independent of the government; membership of the Commission was too limited (five members, three of them part-time) to provide effective national coverage and therefore commissions should be set up at prefectural rather than national level; staff for the secretariat should be selected independently and have human rights expertise; the proposed government powers might result in interference with the freedom of the press and with the activities of organizations such as the BLL; and commissioners should be trained in effective resolution of human rights offences (Tomonaga 2002a). In other words, the commission should be free from government interference, have some real expertise in the area of its remit and be structured in a manner most likely to enable effective responses to civil rights offences.

The government's proposals for revision were opposed not only by the BLL but also by other human rights organizations, the Japan Federation of Bar Associations,[11] the Japan Civil Liberties Union,[12] the Japan PEN Club[13] and mass media organizations. Alternative proposals had also been put forward by the Democratic Party and the Social Democratic Party. A poll conducted by the *Mainichi Shimbun* found that 50 per cent of the House of Representatives and House of Councillors' members thought the Bill should be scrapped (*Mainichi Shimbun* 2002). As we saw in Chapter 1, however, the issue remains unresolved at the time of writing, despite continuing pressure from CERD.

# 4

# ETHNICITY

Ethnicity in Japan, as in other countries, is a favourite target for both outright linguistic slurs and linguistic stereotyping. This chapter will look at three case studies, that of the Ainu people, Japan's ethnic Korean community, and other foreigners, but this list is by no means exclusive. The case studies are intended only to outline the dimensions and nature of the terminology used about these specific groups as a guide to the sort of language protested by ethnic groups in Japan. Okinawans, for example, at the other end of Japan from most Ainu people, have also been targeted, as have Middle Eastern immigrant workers.

## The Ainu people

The Ainu people are Japan's indigenous minority, numbered as of a 1999 survey at 23,767 living in the northern island of Hokkaido alone (Hokkaidō Utari Kyōkai n.d.). This population is self-identified; many, for a variety of reasons, may not have chosen to claim Ainu ethnicity. Nor does it include Ainu people living outside of Hokkaido, estimated to number around 8–10,000. A 2003 newspaper article reported that the Utari Kyōkai (Ainu Association of Hokkaido) estimated the true Ainu population to be around three to four times higher than that reported in the survey (Bogdanowicz 2003). This range suggests 'the complexity of allocating and claiming identities in a society which has for decades sought to eradicate subnational senses of being' (Morris-Suzuki 1998: 183).

When educator and linguist Ueda Kazutoshi spoke so eloquently in 1894 of language as a tool for creating a cohesive nation, he expressed gratitude that Japan, not being a multi-ethnic state, had no need to proscribe the use of other languages within its borders (Ueda 1894: 1–11). It had apparently escaped his attention that the

Ainu, who by that time lived mainly in Hokkaido, were indeed an indigenous minority with a language of their own. Ueda, having returned to Japan only the previous year from postgraduate study in Germany, may be forgiven for this lapse: by 1894, the Ainu had been for 23 years subject to a policy of assimilation ordered by the Meiji government's Hokkaido Reclamation Agency. Under this regime, their homeland was renamed Hokkaido (from its name of Ainu Moshir, 'the earth where the Ainu live'), they were ordered to speak Japanese (which became the language of education, where Ainu was never used) and their cultural practices were proscribed. In Ueda's eyes, therefore, and in the rhetoric of the government of the day, the Ainu were on their way to being assimilated as Japanese, a policy also to be followed in the Imperial colony of Taiwan from 1895.

In the case of Prime Minister Nakasone Yasuhiro, who declared in 1986 that Japan was a 'tan'itsu minzoku' (mono-ethnic nation), however, no such licence could be permitted. By that time indigenous peoples around the world had begun to mobilize under the umbrella of international organizations, notably the United Nations, and it was no longer possible to sustain such a position. Ainu response to Nakasone's comments was immediate: the Kantō Utari Kai (KUK), an association of Ainu people living in the Kanto area in and around Tokyo established in 1980, held a rally to protest, calling it a 'Meeting for the Autonomous Existence of the Ainu People', in November 1986.

Ainu activism, always present in some form but newly energized since the early 1980s, accelerated following Nakasone's remarks. The Utari Kyōkai (AAH) wrote to the United Nations Centre for Human Rights asking for an investigation of the Ainu situation, and sent its first representatives to the United Nations Working Group on Indigenous Populations in 1987. Two years later, in 1989, AAH representatives were further sent to the International Labour Organization (ILO) in support of ILO Treaty 107, which opposed the assimilation of indigenous peoples into dominant cultures. The opinion they proffered ran in part as follows, and made a clear connection with the growing international concern with identity politics:

> As stated in item 2 above, this existing Convention holds integrationism as its basic principle and aims at the protection of the populations concerned, which is undoubtedly an archaic idea, and the application of this principle is destructive. We, therefore, believe that the Convention

should be revised in favour of the respect for identity being its fundamental idea.

This applies to the Ainu people in Japan, too. For . . . the group that, originally living in Hokkaido, Sakhalin, and the Kuriles as the AINU MOSHIRI (the earth where the Ainu live), possesses its own language and culture, has engaged in a common economic life, and has established its own history, is the Ainu people.

(Ainu Association of Hokkaido 1989)

Nomura Giichi, chairman of the AAH, addressing the United Nations General Assembly in December 1992, took wry aim at Nakasone's comments when he reflected on what had ensued:

For we Ainu, who have formed a distinct society and culture in Hokkaido, the Kurile Islands and southern Sakhalin from time immemorial, there is yet another reason why today will have a special significance in our history. This is because up until 1986, a mere six years ago, the government of Japan denied even our very existence in its proud claim that Japan, alone in the world, is a 'mono-ethnic nation.' However, here today, our existence is being clearly recognized by the United Nations itself.

(Nomura 1993: 33)

Though still often not, it would seem, in Japan, where as recently as July 2001 the Minister for Economy, Trade and Industry infuriated Ainu activists by referring to Japan as a nation inhabited by a single race during a speech in Sapporo (*Mainichi Shimbun* 2001b).

The history of the Japanese colonisation of Hokkaido and the subsequent marginalization of the Ainu who lived there is well documented (e.g. Siddle 1996). Prior to the beginning of the Meiji Period (1868–1912) which signalled the beginning of Japan's modern period, the Matsumae clan and Japanese traders in charge of the trading posts for over 200 years instituted procedures such as drafting Ainu men as fishermen in places distant from their villages which led to the fragmentation and decline of the Ainu communities. During this period it was important that Ainu were perceived as non-Japanese, in order to constitute them as the Other, and they were therefore forbidden to speak Japanese or to adopt Japanese dress and practices. 'The demarcation of an "ethnic boundary" . . . between the Ainu and the Japanese was a critical element in determining the political boundaries of the early modern Japanese state' (Howell 1994: 65). Later, within the political and economic framework of an expanding nation which needed to define its northern borders in the face of Russian proximity, it became necessary to assert that the Ainu were indeed Japanese. Soon after the Meiji Restoration, therefore, the Ainu – who, like the Burakumin, had not hitherto appeared on the four-tier class system – were given Japanese citizenship as 'heimin' (commoners) and subjected to a policy of assimilation which saw their language and the practice of many of their customs forbidden and their difference ignored. 'With this, the status of the Ainu was transformed from that of an oppressed racial group into a minority in a modern nation state' (Baba 1980: 63). Under the rubric of 'kaitaku' (development) rather than border defence, the Japanese government encouraged immigration from the south with land grants which saw the disappearance of Ainu hunting grounds at the same time as it forbade the use of traditional hunting methods and encouraged Ainu to engage instead in agriculture.

Ainu people were required to speak Japanese and to use Ainu names under the terms of the Hokkaido Former Aborigines Protection Act of 1899, which stipulated total assimilation: hunter-gathers were to become farmers (albeit on poor tracts of land) and Ainu children were to be educated only in the Japanese language, a move described by Koshida (1993: 3) as a policy of ethnocide which aimed 'to destroy the Ainu's lifestyle and their way of thinking'. For the Ainu people, says activist Chikap Mieko, it was as great a dislocation as if the Japanese of today were suddenly to be told that they would henceforth have to abandon their language to speak English or Russian and adopt the food and customs of the United States and the (then) Soviet Union (Chikap 1991: 162). The word 'Ainu', always a term of disrespect in the eyes of many mainland Japanese and shunned for a long time by the Ainu people themselves on that account, became synonymous with the concept of a dying race, a vanishing people, which was the framework which informed contemporary academic studies.

The 1990s saw a number of significant events. Kayano Shigeru (1926– ) became the first Ainu person to be elected to the *Diet*. A draft Cultural Promotion Act took shape, albeit with minimal Ainu participation (Siddle 2002: 407). A court case brought by two Ainu men (one of whom was Kayano) over the construction of the Nibutani Dam on ancestral lands led to a ruling by the Sapporo District Court in 1997 that the Ainu people fitted the International Covenant on Civil and Political Rights' (ratified by Japan in 1979)

Article 27 definition of a minority. Because this meant recognition of the Ainu people's right to their own culture and language under the Covenant, the Ainu Cultural Promotion Act (CPA), through which the government for the first time recognized the Ainu as an ethnic minority, was enacted on 1 July 1997 and the 1899 Former Aborigines Protection Act was abolished.

The Act promotes understanding and appreciation of Ainu culture and language through providing funds for the activities of the Foundation for Research and Promotion of Ainu Culture, established in 1997, directing government energies to cultural promotion activities rather than addressing issues of rights and compensation. Ainu activists are not happy with the Act, since Ainu culture is defined in terms of Ainu tradition, i.e. difference, with no recognition of the hybridity that is a feature of present-day Ainu culture, as it is of other cultures, or of the Ainu struggle against colonial oppression and discrimination:

> Official Ainu culture is thus limited to language and the creative or artistic production of objects or performances in clearly defined contexts largely divorced from everyday life. One result is that through the emphasis on traditional culture the 'tourist Ainu' (kankō Ainu) has gained an ironic new respectability.
>
> (Siddle 2002: 413)

Even the promotion of Ainu language ignores present-day realities, choosing to equate language with identity without recognizing that most Ainu pour their creative energies into dance and handicrafts rather than Ainu-language cultural production and that in fact most of the Ainu language classes in Hokkaido are attended by Japanese.

Where language is concerned, it is not just today's emphasis on preservation of heritage language or the historical specificities of language controls which have been important in defining Ainu identity. As with the other groups discussed in this book, linguistic stereotyping and use of derogatory terms have also played a crucial part in defining boundaries between Ainu and majority Japanese, as we shall now discover.

### Ainu-related linguistic stereotyping

'The history of the Ainu people has been, in part, a struggle over their discursive representation' (Siddle 2002: 405). The terms regarded as discriminatory by Ainu people are inextricably bound up with the history of their colonization and exploitation, and in particular with their racialization within the terms of empire and their portrayal by both government and academe as a 'dying race'. As with other minorities, Ainu people were subjected to economic deprivation and despised on account of its effects, which led to the name of the entire people being used as a term of abuse.

'The problem of what to call the people – natives, former aborigines, primitives, indigenous people, Ainu-Japanese or even Utari – remains a heated, unsolved subject' (Sala 1975: 63). For many Ainu people, the word 'Ainu' itself, which in the Ainu language means 'human being', was for a long time regarded as something to be avoided because it had become tainted by derogatory connotations in mainstream parlance. Some of those connotations related to the physical: 'Ainu dolls' sold in shops had 'inhuman, exaggerated features' (Totsuka 1993: 13); children were taunted with shouts of 'Ainu! Ainu!', leading to a recognition on their part that '"Ainu" was not a word to be proud of' (Chiri 1993: 19). The name itself lent itself to puns, as 'inu' means dog in Japanese. 'Ainu' could therefore equate to 'A-inu!' (look, a dog!). That this was still a popular taunt even as late as 1986 became clear when Nakasone followed up his earlier remarks about the mono-ethnic nature of Japan with a statement to a parliamentary committee that he did not think minorities in Japan experienced discrimination. The Hokkaido Utari Kyōkai thereupon responded with a list of incidents detailing discrimination against Ainu, one of which involved the 'dog' taunt. In April that same year, a social studies comic book, used as a teaching aid in schools, had been published by a Tokyo press. Children are depicted as saying 'Look, a dog is coming!' when an Ainu child approaches (Roscoe 1986: 67):

> One of the popular racial jokes used against the Ainu is a pseudo-etymological explanation of their origin. In Japanese the phoneme 'a' can indicate 'second best', while 'inu' is the Japanese word for 'dog'. It is therefore not difficult to see how the Ainu were denigrated by the Japanese through this pseudo-etymological link with dogs and how this deliberate misinterpretation of a foreign language could then be used by the dominant power group as a rationalisation for relegating the Ainu to an inferior status.
>
> (Taira 1996)

Others equated the word 'Ainu' with poverty and stupidity, never acknowledging the role of mainstream Japanese in bringing about that poverty and consequent reduced access to education. 'Primitive', too, has been a favoured connotation and remains so even today in some quarters: a home page purporting to offer an alphabetical introduction (in English) to the multiple faces of Japan, after first remarking on the 'abundant black hair and long strong beards' of Ainu people, goes on to describe them in a pop-up box as 'primitive people', whose main occupation is fishing and farming and who may be seen 'in their native surroundings' at a tourist village in Hokkaido (no author given 1997). This harks back to the 'tourist Ainu' stereotype unacceptable to Ainu activists but is promoted unexamined on a site purporting to educate visitors from outside Japan. Terms such as 'kankō Ainu' are inextricably linked with historical moments for their status as derogatory terms early in the twentieth century.

A chronology of Ainu-Japanese contact given in a special issue of *AMPO* devoted to the topic records:

> 1960: A meeting for the reconstruction of the AAH (Ainu Association of Hokkaido) is held. The following year its Japanese name is changed to the Hokkaido Utari Association (the English translation is not changed). The reason for the change is that some Ainu are uneasy with the word 'Ainu,' which recalls a history of discrimination. They decide to use the word 'utari,' which means 'fellow,' in its place.
>
> (No author given 1993: 27)

'Utari', notes Sala (1975: 56) in relation to this decision, 'thus became a euphemism, an indication among other things that the term Ainu (which means "man" or "human being") had become an unendurable burden in a highly prejudiced society'.

The 1970s, however, saw 'Ainu' incorporated into several names, among them the Nibutani Ainu Cultural Resource Museum, the Yay Yukar Ainu Minzoku Gakkai (Acting Ainu Ethnological Society) and a 'National Meeting of the Talking Ainu' in 1973 (Koshida 1993: 5). Koshida sees this as an 'amazing event', one which can be seen as a 'declaration to live fully as human beings'. He cites Hiramura Akemi, one of the editors of an Ainu opinion paper *Anutar Ainu* (*We Human Beings*, 1973–76) on this matter:

I was very surprised when I read a letter in a newspaper saying that since the word 'Ainu' was a discriminatory term, it should be abolished. What surprised me even more was that the writer was an Ainu. But I should not be surprised . . . Some people insist on the word 'utari', which means 'fellows' or 'mates'. But this is only used inside Ainu society. There's no reason for the Japanese to call us utari. Why is it that Ainu have also come to internalize these definitions of the mainstream Japanese? . . . We should reclaim the word 'Ainu' from the dirtiness it has gotten in the eyes of the discriminators, and take it as our own. Otherwise, the word 'Ainu' will lose its original meaning.

'Ainu', then, is a good example of a term used in a derogatory manner by a dominant section of society being reclaimed by its owners as a marker of ethnic pride, a trend which emerged in the 1980s along with the growth of an 'Ainu nation' consciousness fostered by young activists intent on dispelling the prevailing image of the Ainu as a 'dying race' (Siddle 1996: 24).

Takagi (1999: 176–9) devotes a mere four pages to discussion of Ainu-related linguistic discrimination in his study of discriminatory language and minority groups, compared to a whole chapter each on both Burakumin and people with disabilities. The reason for this probably lies in the lack of organized protests from Ainu groups until relatively late, not until after the formation in 1972 of the Ainu Liberation League with its resonances with the BLL and their strategy of denunciation campaigns against the media. Takagi's discussion deals initially with the Nakasone incident detailed above and its aftermath, but goes on to list a few instances of derogatory language used in the mass media and in books. In July 1981, for example, the Japan Travel Bureau (JTB), in an advertisement in the English-language *Japan Times* for travel in Hokkaido, used the word 'kebukai' (hairy) to describe Ainu people. This prompted local Ainu people to convene a denunciation meeting and protest to the JTB. The JTB inserted an apology in the newspaper, removed all derogatory references to Ainu from its Hokkaido guidebook and agreed to educate all staff (a Burakumin pattern). This incident was further referred to in a submission by the AAH to the Sixth Session of the Working Group on Indigenous Populations in Geneva in 1988 (Ainu Association of Hokkaido 1988) and is often referred to in scholarly literature on the Ainu (e.g. Hanazaki 1996: 127–8; Siddle 1997: 32). The AAH submission noted that 'there was and is no domestic law in Japan that can effectively regulate racially discriminatory advertisements by invoking the International Convention on the Elimination of All Forms of Racial Discrimination, as the Japanese government has not ratified it'. As we saw in Chapter 1, Japan has since ratified the Convention, but the existence of such a law remains a sticking point in its accession.

The significance of the insult 'hairy', which refers to the fact that pure-blooded Ainu people have more body hair than do Japanese, lies in its animal associations: taunts of 'monkey' were often to be heard on that account. Writer Ishimori Nobuo's *Kotan no Kuchibue* (*A Whistle in the Ainu Village*) includes a scene in which an Ainu child agonizes over having to expose her hairy body to her Japanese friend in the bath and eventually attempts to kill herself before her father's grave (Yumoto 1963, cited in Taira 1996). Ainu activist Ogawa Sanae resorted to bleaching the hair on her small daughter's legs after another child's mother recommended a daily bath to remove the 'dust' on her legs (Taira 1996). This association of hairiness with animals and dirt had also found expression in the early descriptions of Europeans as hairy barbarians.

Victorian writers perpetuated the linked use of the words 'hairy' and 'Ainu'. Christian missionary John Batchelor, who worked in Hokkaido, published *The Ainu of Japan: The Religions, Superstitions and General History of the Hairy Aborigines of Japan* in 1892, and adventurer A.H. Savage Landor published a travelogue with the title of *Alone with the Hairy Ainu* the following year. Landor describes the Ainu throughout his book as 'savages', 'barbarians' and 'the hairy people'. McGee (1904: 1–2) describes how at the St Louis World's Fair in 1904 the Outdoor Anthropology Exhibit classified the 'hairy Ainu' as among 'the most peculiar peoples in the world'; their village reservation (along with several others) in the outdoor section of the exhibit 'presents the race narrative of odd people who mark time while the world advances . . . In brief, one may learn in the indoor exhibit how our own prehistoric forbears lived, and then see, outside, people untouched by the march of progress still living in similar crude manner'.

'In every rural district, there are still Japanese who make derogatory comments or show contempt for their Ainu neighbours. Nineteenth-century images of the "hairy, dirty, shōchū-drinking natives" still are widespread' (Sala 1975: 49). The list of anti-Ainu discriminatory incidents compiled by the AAH in 1986 included information about Ainu women wanting to become nurses being told to shave their hairy arms when they applied for hospital jobs

(Roscoe 1986: 67). Indeed, Prime Minister Nakasone himself, trying to extricate himself from a sticky situation with a joke, told the
parliamentary committee on that occasion that his own bushy eye-
brows and dark beard meant he probably had Ainu blood himself.
Hair, then, was not a good thing to have in Japan, and 'kebukai'
applied to Ainu people came to encapsulate all that was undesirable
in terms of both physical and mental characteristics. As Taira (1996)
notes, 'this reputed duality [of hairiness vs. comparatively non-hairy
Japanese] is turned into the relative worth of each race by the ideology of the dominant'. The link between hairiness and barbarian
status was strong, and words such as 'ijin', 'iteki' (both meaning
'barbarian') and 'Ezo' (Eastern barbarian) were often used when
speaking of Ainu people (Siddle 1996: 5) in both official reports and
travellers' tales. 'Whereas the former stereotypes [of Ainu under
Matsumae rule] developed in association with the ruling class ideology, the newly formed anti-Ainu prejudice emerged more widely
at the popular level' (Baba 1980: 70).

'Barbarian' was a term weighted with particular significance both
in Japan's premodern period and during the Meiji Period. Early con-
tacts with Europeans had earned them the designation of 'nanban'
(southern barbarians), often linked with an associated description
of 'hairy' or 'red-haired'. All hairy people, it seemed, or at least those
hairier than the Japanese, were automatically designated barbarians.
Barbarians were those on the periphery, with Europeans the 'outer
barbarians' of a series of concentric circles emanating outwards
from Japan. This view stemmed originally from 'the Chinese
Hua-yi (in Japanese ka-i) model of the world, in which barbarism
increases the farther one moves away from the settled and civilized
centre (ka)' (Morris-Suzuki 1998: 15). The centre of the circles in
the original model was of course China; Morris-Suzuki traces the
development of the Japanese version in which the centre became
with increasing degrees of confidence Japan, so that by the beginning
of the Tokugawa Period the Tokugawa Shogunate was engaged in
reconceptualizing relationships between the centre of power in Edo
(today's Tokyo) and Japan's outer boundaries, among them the
northern island now called Hokkaido and the southern kingdom of
the Ryūkyūs. If the people living on the peripheries in this particular set of circles emanating out from Edo – the Ainu in the north
and the people of the Ryūkyūs in the south – were to be properly
constituted in their role as outer-circle barbarians subject to Japanese
control, it was important that they be seen as different. Hence the
emphasis on the hirsuteness of the Ainu, an exotic physical marker

of difference from the smoother-skinned 'wajin' (mainland Japanese) which underlined their status as barbarians and marked them out as 'beyond the realms of the existing social order' (Morris-Suzuki 1998: 19). That the term 'hairy' today is offensive to Ainu people stems not only from its association with dogs and other animals but also from its role in delineating them as barbarians beyond the civilized pale.

Thanks to the history of assimilation and oppression represented by the 1899 Former Aborigines Protection Act (Hokkaidō Kyūdojin Hogohō), 'former aborigine' (kyūdojin) is another loaded term, which has in some areas been expunged from family registers (Sala 1975: 63). As often happens when one particular group is marked out for special treatment of this kind, the Law 'tended to strengthen Wajin prejudice against the Ainu as a protected – and therefore "different" – race' (Baba 1980: 74). Ainu groups had been calling for the repeal of this law since early in the Showa Period (1926–89), on the grounds that its paternalistic provisions hindered their efforts to become self-sufficient.

## Language protests

The main all-Ainu (as opposed to Japanese and Ainu) association is the Hokkaido Utari Kyōkai (Ainu Association of Hokkaido), established in 1946 in order to advance Ainu interests in the face of discrimination. The leadership has favoured advancement through assimilation and social welfare, i.e. proceeding on the Japanese government's terms relating to the 'protection' of Ainu rather than backing confrontational actions designed to establish a separate Ainu identity. Subsidized by the Hokkaido prefectural govern-ment, the Association's major activities have included educational, medical and cultural projects as well as campaigns to reclaim land for Ainu use (Baba 1980: 78). While the emphasis of this group was therefore on reconciliation rather than militant protest, it did take issue with language now and then. In 1972, for example, as the result of a protest from the AAH, a Hokkaido Broadcasting Company TV programme was cancelled and an apology issued, and 6,300 copies of the Japanese version of *Playboy* were recalled (again with an apology) because they included a discriminatory cartoon (Siddle 1997: 32).

Much more active has been the Ainu Liberation League, formed by Ainu activist Yūki Shōji in 1972 under the influence of the BLL. Organized protest by Burakumin had been watched from the early stages by some Ainu people: when young poet Iboshi Hokuto (1902–29) heard of the Suiheisha Sengen ('Levellers' Declaration) in 1922, for example, it inspired him to leave Tokyo and return to Hokkaido in order to reassert his Ainu identity. A *tanka* poem, which reads in translation 'I aspire to give the new, worthy concept of Ainu to the people of the mainland', echoes the Suiheisha declaration of pride in the name 'eta' (Hanazaki 1996: 122). It was not Ainu people themselves that Iboshi sought to make proud of the name 'Ainu', however, but the mainstream Japanese whom he wished to impress with it.

Yūki formed the Ainu Liberation League along the lines of the BLL because he was impatient with the assimilationist emphasis of the Utari Kyōkai, of which he had been a member of the board of directors, and sought more direct action which would foster Ainu minority politics and pride in Ainu identity. Perhaps the best-known activity of the Liberation League was the Burakumin-style denunciation carried out at an academic conference of anthropologists and folklorists in Sapporo in August 1972, when Yūki and others unexpectedly commandeered the podium to take issue with the academic practices of treating Ainu as relics of a dying race and ignoring the way they lived in modern Japan. Siddle (1993: 44) records a further instance of denunciation in 1977 when Yūki and a large group of students at Hokkaido University penned up in his office a recalcitrant professor who had made derogatory statements about Ainu in his lectures and refused to apologize. Riot police were called in to free the professor. When several months later a formal request for an apology was ignored, Yūki and others staged a sit-in at the university, pitching tents in the snow for three weeks until the professor agreed to attend two long days of denunciation meetings and eventually apologized. During the sit-in, representatives of Burakumin organizations visited to offer support. Such denunciation tactics, Siddle concludes, may result only in deepening the silence surrounding sensitive issues, since scholars and publishers are reluctant to engage in discussion of such issues for fear of reprisals (as is the case with the press in general).

Following the 1993 United Nations Year for Indigenous People, Ainu activism against linguistic slurs increased on a variety of fronts, including both non-fiction and fiction books (including children's literature) and TV shows. The name used to refer to them was not an issue this time, as the media had earlier decided to use the term 'Ainu minzoku' (Ainu people) when referring to Ainu after a complaint in 1989 from the Ainu Liberation League over the appearance of the word 'Ainu-kei gyomin' (fishermen of Ainu descent) in an *Asahi Shimbun* report on crab poaching. The *Asahi* published an apology a week later. 'Ainu-kei', the League felt, with its overtones of the period of forced assimilation, was an affront to their ethnic pride. The media settled on 'Ainu minzoku' because the word 'Ainu' itself means 'human being' in the Ainu language; to say 'Ainujin' (Ainu people) or 'Ainu no hitotachi' (Ainu people) would therefore be redundant, while to say 'Ainu' alone sounded disrespectful to some (Yamanaka 1995: 69–72). With the terminology thus settled, attention was turned to other types of language and stereotyping.

In early 1991, following a reissue of a 1982 book called *Kita no Jinmeiroku* (*Who's Who of the North*) which contained the statement that the Ainu dog was used for food, the president of the AAH complained that the Ainu had never eaten dogs and that moreover the name 'Ainu inu' (Ainu dog) itself was discriminatory. Although the author and his publisher (Shinchōsha) agreed to excise the passage from any future editions, the publisher forgot to do so, with the result that in 1993 another complaint was made. This time the publisher not only apologized but recalled the books in order to take out the passage and insert an apology at the end of the book (Gekkan 'Tsukuru' Henshūbu 1995: 336–7).

1994 was a very active year. On New Year's Day, Nihon Terebi broadcast a show featuring popular host Beat Takeshi in which nine 'talents' from a theatre company dressed up and did a mocking dance to the tune 'Night of the Iyomante'. The Iyomante is a ceremony sacred to the Ainu people in which the soul of a bear is returned to the country of the gods. Representatives of three different Ainu rights groups visited the channel and expressed their anger over the great insult offered to the Ainu people by this mocking representation of the ceremony, whereat the Nihon Terebi management at once offered a written apology (Takagi 1999: 177–8) and apologized on air a week later. A month after that, the AAH complained to publisher Kobunsha that a reprint of a 1942 novel *Ainu no Gakkō* (*The Ainu School*) was full of 50-year-old expressions which were derogatory to Ainu people, who were depicted as appearing mean and servile. Kobunsha apologized, and decided to print no further copies and to recall those already in circulation. Then a children's story, also 50 years old, included in supplementary teaching material for morals classes, drew complaint because it misrepresented the Ainu people and their culture, thus perpetuating discrimination and bias. A particular focus of complaint was the use of the word 'shūchō' (chieftain),[1] which, they said, did not apply to the Ainu. The publisher, Gakken, decided to replace the story with something else (Gekkan 'Tsukuru' Henshūbu 1995: 340).

The effectiveness of denunciation, or even the threat of denunciation and protest rallies by noisy activists, is demonstrated by how quickly these protests brought forth apologies and in some cases redress through recall of publications on the part of the media. It became apparent that Hokkaido, isolated from the Burakumin denunciations of media on the mainland by virtue of the fact that it was not an area where numbers of Burakumin lived, was no longer quarantined but faced similar activism from its own local people. Self-censorship on the part of national media or publishing houses was the automatic response. Yamanaka (1995: 72) saw in that a worrying harbinger of the kind of blackout of discussion of Ainu issues which pertained to Burakumin issues in the press: if the 'kotobagari' and 'sakuhingari' (works-hunts) incidents led publishers to avoid the famous works of the past and if the Ainu developed an image as strong and hard like Burakumin, the result would be no mass media exposure at all.

## The ethnic Korean population

In 2002, there were 625,422 resident-alien ethnic Koreans (known as *zainichi kankokujin*, or *zainichi* for short) living in Japan, accounting for a third of the total foreign population (Ministry of Justice 2003) and making them Japan's largest minority group after the Burakumin and the Okinawans. These figures do not include those Koreans who have taken Japanese citizenship. Many are third- and fourth-generation residents, whose families either came to Japan in search of employment during the period when Korea was a Japanese colony (1910–45) or were forcibly brought there during the war to work. After the war, many of those in the earlier wave, having assimilated to Japan, chose not to return to Korea even though they lost their Japanese citizenship at that time. In addition to long-term residents of Japan, who may or may not have taken citizenship and who may be affiliated with either North or South Korean, the Korean population also encompasses young job-seeking newcomers from South Korea (Okano and Tsuchiya 1999: 111–12) and is clustered in large urban centres such as Tokyo and Osaka.

Like the Ainu people, Koreans have been subject to many forms of discrimination in employment, education and marriage. In the early twentieth century, during Japan's colonization of Korea, they consistently ranked alongside Burakumin as the despised Other (Fowler 2000: 17). Korean residents were murdered (some by police) in the wake of the 1923 Kantō earthquake when rumours spread that they were lighting fires and looting; as a result, after the 1995 Hanshin earthquake, many of the large Korean community in the area were reluctant to accept help from the authorities, fearing a repeat. Today, school bullying of Korean children has been widely reported: a survey of students by Kim (n.d.) found that 30 per cent of respondents remembered experiences of bullying in the upper years of primary school. Abundant evidence exists of landlords refusing to rent apartments to people on the basis of a Korean-sounding name or a confirmed Korean identity. As discussed in Chapter 1, Korean students are regularly harassed during times of overt friction between Japan and North Korea. Even in the area of sexualities, 'many Japanese think that gays in Japan are in fact not Japanese but Korean' (Valentine 1997: 81), i.e. those foreigners ( = not us) are at it again.

Until very recently, children whose parents chose to have them educated at Korean community schools were not allowed to apply to enter national universities because they had not gone through the standard Japanese education system.[2] This created the anomalous situation whereby a student from Korea could apply for entrance to a prestigious national university and be accepted as an international student, but a Korean-background student who had grown up in Japan, spoke Japanese as their first language and had been educated in Japan, albeit at a non-government school, could not (Tanaka 1991: 164–6 cited in Sugimoto 2003). Although from April 2004 the rules were changed to permit graduates of all foreign schools in Japan to sit for university entrance examinations, including the 1,000 or so students who graduate from Korean schools each year, even then the decision to include Koreans did not come easily. The original decision, announced in March 2003, that only graduates of foreign schools affiliated with Europe or America could do so was expanded to include them after complaints that the original plan was racist.

Koreans were made to take Japanese names during the colonial period, and most in Japan still use Japanese names today even though it is no longer mandatory. 'It is assumed that over 80% of young Koreans pass as Japanese in their daily life by using Japanese names, except when they tell their secret to close Japanese friends' (Fukuoka 1996). The common Korean surname Kim is written with the character 金, read 'kane' in Japanese, and many

Koreans took Japanese surnames which incorporated that element (e.g. Kaneyama, Kaneda). This played a part in identifying (and eliminating) Korean applicants for jobs in the employment black-lists circulated among large companies and discussed in Chapter 3. In a collection of actual identity check reports reproduced by the BLL, a surname containing the character 金 was underlined; then, after further checks confirmed that the owner of the name was not in fact of Korean ancestry, the words 'Nihonjin' and 'OK' (Japanese – OK) were written on the paper (Buraku Liberation League 1998). Despite the success of a 1974 court case settled in favour of a young Korean man who had satisfied Hitachi's entry requirements using his Japanese name but was refused employment when Hitachi learned he was Korean, employment discrimination in the corporate sector remains a factor. While there have been cases during the 1990s of young Koreans have been employed in major firms, in other instances people have lost their jobs when their employers discovered their ethnic origin.

## Language and Koreans

In addition to derogatory descriptions of Koreans, the manner in which Koreans living in Japan are designated has also been contentious, owing to the historical connotations of oppression or political division inherent in these terms. The usual word for North Korea is 'chōsen'; for South Korea, 'kankoku'. To call Koreans 'chōsenjin' is felt by many (both Koreans and Japanese alike) to be discriminatory because of the overtones it acquired during the period when Korean was Japan's colony; 'kankokujin', on the other hand, refers only to South Koreans, while many of Japan's ethnic Korean population identify with North Korea. When NHK, the national public broadcaster, speaks of Korean residents it conflates both terms into 'zainichi kankoku-chōsenjin', another example of a bureaucratic solution aimed at avoiding offence which results in an awkward expression not likely to form part of everyday use (Valentine 1998: 6.7).

Over the last decade or so, an increasingly used alternative has been the English word 'Korean' written in katakana. 'Zainichi korian' is the term used in the *Buraku Liberation News*, for example. It also features in the title of a 1995 book, *Zainichi Korian no Aidentiti to Hōteki Chi-i* (*Identity and Legal Position of Ethnic Koreans in Japan*), by Kim Kyong-Duk. Anthropologist Diane Hoffman writes of this trend:

Some explain the usage by saying that it avoids the necessity of making a disctinction (inherent in other terminology) between North and South Koreans. It is more likely, however, that the term reflects awareness of a more modern Korea, as well as more modern notions of Korean identity and ethnicity . . . The term has a distinctly modern tone that overcomes past images associated with the Korean minority in Japan, including disparaged cultural and social identity and political polarization . . . In this way, the young Korean minority's relations with Japanese society are tacitly re-defined so as to eliminate the former disparaged status. In this sense, the term reflects the emergence of a new form of identity for Koreans in Japan that moves beyond the old boundaries and categories of host and minority, Japanese and Korean.

(Hoffman 1992: 482, 487)

This is a valid argument. Much of this change in image during the 1990s, in a move away from the former North-South politically polarized forms of identification, is due to the popularity of Korean popular culture in Japan and other associated factors: a gourmet boom which has prompted interest in Korean cuisine, and an ethnic boom where Asia is seen as cool. Korean singers, journalists, news-readers and writers became much more visible during the 1990s (Maher 1995a: 99), and in late 2004 we witnessed the extraordinary spectacle of 5,000 middle-aged women, many of them screaming like teenagers over a pop star, besieging Korean actor Bae Yong-Joon during his visit to Tokyo (Alford 2004). Ryang (2002: 6, n. 9) agrees that popular culture is a driving force: whereas in the past movies by *zainichi* Koreans always focused on the national past and issues of national identity, 'in the 1990s, with the production of new types of movies . . . the entertainment value of *zainichi* cultural products increased against the background of the "multiculturalist" discourse that was rapidly emerging in Japan in the face of the influx of foreign workers'. With a new visibility not predicated on past historical events or current politics, therefore, the term 'korian' very much signifies a change in self-perception of identity among young Koreans today.

This can only be a good thing. The word 'senjin' (short for 'Chōsenjin') is a source of great bitterness because of the freight of derogatory overtones it carries, having been created as a term of ethnic contempt for Koreans under Japanese imperialism following the annexation of Korea by Japan. It is widely recognized as discriminatory (Isomura and Fukuoka 1994: 24), and has been compared with the practice in English of using the derogatory abbreviation 'Jap' for 'Japanese' (Valentine 1998: n. 12). Another abbreviation considered highly derogatory is 'hokusen', which uses the characters for 'north' and the second character in the word 'chōsen' but not the first, i.e. 北鮮 rather than 北朝鮮. A defendant in a case being heard by the Nagoya High Court in 1995 was shocked when the judge used this term when enquiring about a person's nationality, and was even more offended when the court official answered and the trial proceeded without comment. He found it unbelievable that 50 years after the war, in a Japan at last beginning to take heed of its invasion of Asian countries, a high court judge would use the word 'hokusen'. The *Asahi Shimbun's* 1994 list of words to be avoided had warned against dropping the first syllable of 'chōsen' because Japanese government personnel had done that to display contempt during the colonial period, on the grounds that since Koreans were a headless ( = brainless) race it made sense to delete the first (head) syllable of their name. Yet a judge was using this term, known to be discriminatory, in a supposedly impartial court in 1995 in a case involving Korean residents (no author given 1995).

Anti-Korean graffiti feature from time to time in public places. The Buraku Kaihō Kenkyūkai (Buraku Liberation Study Group) at Osaka University, for example, reported finding 'to the right of the light switch just after you get out of the sixth floor elevator' in the Languages and Cultures building the phrases (all written in katakana) 'Chōsenjin suzu o kubi ni tsukete aruke, oto ga kikoetara sugu ni wakaru' (Koreans, walk with bells round your necks so we'll know when we hear the sound). The web page on which the report appeared reproduced the graffiti and commented on the unfavourable effect such a phrase would be likely to have on both Korean residents and international students from Korea studying at the university. This was not the first time such things had happened at the university, the group reported: between 1990 and 1993, many such anti-Korean and anti-Burakumin scribblings had been found. The latest effort had read 'Kill the Koreans etc.'. Similar graffiti had been found at other universities in the city as well, providing evidence for those who cared to look that discrimination was alive and well and near at hand. The group called on the university to adopt a more positive stance and to offer a course in human rights education which covered all minority groups, not just Burakumin and Koreans (Osaka Daigaku Buraku Kaihō Kenkyūkai n.d.).

Universities were not the only place where Koreans could expect to encounter abuse. Wetherall (1981: 290) relates the case of ethnic Korean postwar baseball star Harimoto Isao (Chang Hun), who experienced as a child and later also on the baseball field such jeers as 'ninnikubara' (garlic belly), 'kimuchi kutabare' (kimchi, i.e. Korean, go to hell!) and of course the ubiquitous 'Chōsen ni kaere' (go back to Korea).

The 'chon' part of the word 'bakachon' (foolproof, used in regard to point-and-click cameras) is widely believed to refer to Koreans, although it may not originally have done so at all: Isomura and Fukuoka (1994: 32–3) suggest that it originated in Tokugawa Period popular fiction as a rhetorical synonym for 'fool' (baka), with the phrase 'baka demo chon demo' being abbreviated to 'bakachon'. Many younger people, however, believe that it does indeed refer to Koreans, perhaps as an abbreviation of the discriminatory word 'chonkō' used of students in Korean schools. Utsumi *et al.* (1986: 166) found 'chon' to be the term most commonly used by high-school students to refer to Koreans: 71 per cent of students in a 1981 survey said that they had used that word (34 per cent of them said they thought it demeaned Koreans, 38 per cent that it was just an abbreviation with no intent to demean). Just as many others, however, profess not to know that the term refers to Koreans at all and, upon having it brought to their attention, remark that not knowing means that they meant no discrimination in using the term. This is undeniably true, but Ryang (2002: 10) is not inclined to let people off on that account:

> The occurrence of such incidents is widely reported. Unlike displays of brute racism, these are even more difficult to deal with precisely because the perpetrators mean well and their 'crime' is one of more forgetfulness or simple lack of knowledge. Here the responsibility to learn is totally dismissed, as if it is the responsibility of Koreans, the under-privileged group, to educate the privileged Japanese.

Not everyone agrees with the idea of even Japanese trying to educate other Japanese, let alone Koreans. From time to time internet discussions veer off topic when a member of the discussion group, which may be on any topic, takes exception to the use by another member of a particular term. An example of this in relation to 'bakachon' occurred on a Linux users' discussion group in 1999,[3] when one contributor commented that TurboLinux, used on a regular basis, was 'bakachon' easy. Another contributor took issue with the use of this word, pointing out that it came with historical baggage of racial contempt and should not be used in such a forum, where it was quite possible that it could be read in Korea and give offence. He was not practising 'kotobagari', he insisted: if the former contributor had deliberately used it knowing of its historical baggage, well, that is another point of view, but he himself, although he used to use the word – because after all it is a convenient word – no longer did so after he found out about its associations. A third person took issue with the second: he had never been aware of any historical associations, was there any basis for this in fact, and nobody reading the original sentence would take it that way: was it not perhaps just the interlocutor who did so? It went against the grain of the list, he continued, to have this kind of baseless off-topic 'kotobagari' interpolated: contributors should not be pulled up every time someone used the word 'baka' or 'kichigai'. Words themselves are not discriminatory: even substitute euphemisms can be used in a discriminatory way. The only thing that counts is the intent of the user. This contributor finished by saying that on another list, rather than engaging in baseless 'kotobagari' which restricted people's thoughts, they had combated discrimination head-on, using whatever language they pleased. A final message before the discussion thread petered out reported dictionary research which revealed no connection between Koreans and the use of 'bakachon'. The members of the group, then, or at least those who contributed to the discussion, were robustly against the notion of restrictions on language in their internet dealings, regardless of where the list was read.

The term which has caused the most offence to the Korean community in recent years, and has been most vigorously protested by them, is 'sangokujin' (third country people), a derogatory term used to refer to people of Taiwanese and Korean descent since Japan's colonial period. Tokyo Governor Ishihara Shintarō said in a speech to the Ground Self-Defence Forces in April 2000 that they should be prepared for 'sangokujin' and illegal immigrants to stage riots should a major natural disaster such as an earthquake occur: 'atrocious crimes have been committed again and again by "sangokujin" and other foreigners. We can expect them to riot in the event of a disastrous earthquake'. 'Ishihara warns that foreigners likely to riot after big quake', ran the headline in the *Japan Times* on 11 April 2000. The Chinese and Korean communities were angered not only by his conflation of themselves with undesirable illegal immigrants but also because, in the case of the Korean community, many Koreans had been murdered following the 1923 earthquake.

Ishihara is well-known to be anti-foreigner and is often in the news for making contentious comments of this type. His remark caused a hurricane of comment in newspaper and journal articles and in online chat rooms. The ethnic communities affected censured Ishihara, as did members of labour unions and NGOs who assist foreign workers and residents (McLaughlin 2000), groups of scholars[4] and the Japan Committee of the BLL's international arm, IMADR. The last of these sent a letter pointing out the international conventions to which Japan was signatory that Ishihara's remark contravened and demanding a retraction and apology.[5] A group of celebrities including a third-generation Korean businesswoman held a press conference to demand Ishihara's resignation, while another group of around 40 people from local assemblies and civic groups held a protest rally in a yard at the metropolitan government building.[6] The Tokyo Overseas Chinese Federation held a special meeting to protest strongly against the governor's remarks (*People's Daily* 2000).

Governor Ishihara subsequently denied that he had meant to single out the Chinese and Korean communities and said he had really meant to target illegal immigrants, who he believed to be a significant source of crime, particularly snakeheads from China. He blamed the media for focusing on that one word 'sangokujin' and overlooking the remainder of his remark. As we saw in Chapter 2, he had recourse to the dictionary, noting that the 'sangokujin' entry does not carry any warning that it is derogatory. He did, however, concede that he would not use it again, given the sensitivity of Korean residents in particular to the term.

Several right-wing academics and commentators defended Ishihara as a victim of 'kotobagari' following this incident. A consistent theme in their arguments, notes Morris-Suzuki (2001), was that the word 'sangokujin' is not discriminatory because 'it was introduced during the postwar occupation period as a technical term to describe people from "third countries" other than Japan and the occupying powers', thereby ignoring the historical freight which words acquire depending on the circumstances in which they are used. By using this word, she contends, Ishihara is engaging in an old strategy beloved of politicians of all stripes everywhere, i.e. tapping into xenophobic fears to divert attention from other issues at hand by eliding the old term 'sangokujin' with the more recent phenomenon of 'illegal immigrants' to create one threatening foreign face against which Japanese would be well advised to buffer themselves. The danger is not that Ishihara will really call out the troops to control foreigners but that his remarks and those of his supporters could contribute to undoing the nascent acceptance of diversity in Japanese society.

## Other ethnicities

Numerous other ethnic groups exist in Japan, such as the Okinawan and Brazilian Nikkeijin minorities, but they have not attracted as much attention in terms of public discussion of derogatory language as the two aspects I shall examine in the last section of this discussion on ethnicity and language: namely, the Chinese community and the use of the word 'gaijin' to refer to foreigners.

In 2002 there were 424,282 Chinese people living in Japan (Ministry of Justice 2003), most of them in large cities in the Tokyo-Yokohama conurbation, the Kansai region of western Japan and parts of Southern Kyushu (Maher 1995b: 126). Early immigrants settled in Yokohama, Nagasaki and Kobe; the Chinatown in Yokohama is the world's oldest and largest (Chang 1998). Many of the Chinese community now live outside the Chinatown areas to which Chinese were originally confined in the early Meiji Period and work in the professions, or own restaurants or food-industry businesses. Schools teaching in Japanese and Chinese, which like the Korean schools were until recently not accredited by the government for university entrance exams, educate the children of the postwar wave of Chinese immigrants from Taiwan, although many children attend mainstream Japanese schools.

In general, the resident Chinese community has been subjected to a considerable amount of stereotyping through references to imputed involvement in crime. The US Department of State country report on Japan in 2000 noted:

> There is a widespread perception that many crimes are committed by foreigners. In May the governor of Tokyo stated publicly that foreigners in the country might riot after an earthquake and warned that the country's self defense forces should be prepared. In December the Tokyo police admitted that as part of an anticrime effort, 700 posters, which ultimately were not used, had been issued to police stations to post in the Tokyo area that noted the increase in crime among foreigners, particularly among Chinese, and that urged citizens to call the police if they heard persons speaking Chinese.

The Miwa Company, Japan's largest lock maker, even ran an advertising campaign in 1999 guaranteeing their locks' effectiveness against the face of 'Chinese theft gangs' which maintained 'secret bases' in Japan (French 1999).

With the exception of 'sangokujin', probably the most contested word relating to China and Chinese people is 'shina'. Fogel (1995: 68–71) traces the genealogy of this term, which by the late nineteenth century had moved from being the most commonly used Japanese word for China to the only Japanese term for China. The term came to be seen as highly derogatory, despite not having originally been considered so at all. It regularly features in the 'iikaeshū' lists as a word to be avoided in public discourse. To Chinese people it is redolent of Japanese imperialism, and after Japan's defeat in the war the Japanese government agreed to use 'Chūgoku' (China) instead (Fogel 1995: 75).

In July 2000, the *Nippon Keizai Shimbun* reported that a lecture critical of the Nanjing Massacre had been abandoned after a complaint from an international student in a political science class about the use of the word 'shina', which the student felt was discriminatory. The university issued a counterstatement in which it was careful to point out that the staff member had been removed from teaching that particular class not because of any disputes about the veracity of the Nanjing Massacre itself but because the staff member had consistently refused, despite repeated official requests, to stop using 'shina' in class. The word has been described as encapsulating a world view of 'the superiority of a modern Japan over an unchanging China' (Tanaka 1993: 9), which modern Japan still holds today. Despite the staff member's contention that 'shina' was a contemporary word which was in no way contemptuous of China or Chinese people, the university authorities held to the line that their practice had been always to follow the Ministry of Education's request that this word not be used and assigned the class to someone else. The newspaper report, the official statement assured the public, had wrongly given the reason as being a dispute over the Nanjing facts, but the university upheld the principles of academic freedom and would not remove a lecturer on those grounds; it was rather the language itself that was at issue.

The final word I want to talk about here is 'gaijin' (foreigner), a blanket term applied in theory to foreigners but meaning in practice Caucasians. 'Gaijin', written with characters meaning 'outside person', is a contraction of 'gaikokujin' (person from a foreign country). The latter is the official legal term used to refer to anyone who does not have Japanese citizenship, and has replaced 'gaijin', which can have derogatory overtones particularly when (as often happens) it is preceded by the adjective 'hen na' (weird), in public discourse. 'Gaijin' appears in the 'iikaeshū' and has practically disappeared from the mass media, though not from everyday conversation. Foreigners with sufficient Japanese to recognize the word when they hear it used to refer to them in the street have complained since the 1970s, but there are ways around this: 'less known to the paranoid foreigner is the occasional rendering of "gaijin" as "jingai" to give it both a more secretive and pejorative character' (Wetherall and de Vos 1975).

The website of ISSHO Kikaku, an NGO established in 1992,[7] contains much information on the debate over this word, as does that of David Aldwinckle (Japanese name Arudō Debito), a long-term resident of Japan who has taken Japanese citizenship.[8] In 1996, in response to a TV show in which TV-Asahi News presenter Kume Hiroshi announced that he preferred 'gaijin' to speak poor Japanese rather than to be fluent, ISSHO organized a polite minority group protest. An open letter was sent to the station asking whether it considered 'gaijin' a fit word to broadcast and if so, why, given that it was now hardly ever encountered in media of any kind (ISSHO 1996). The group subsequently carried out an online survey about the use of the word 'gaijin' with the intent of presenting the findings on a follow-up News Station programme. A preliminary analysis of responses received in the first week of the survey was made available online. Nearly 40 per cent of respondents considered the word 'gaijin' to be a discriminatory or racist term; 32.5 per cent did not; and the remaining 27.6 per cent did not know. Of these same respondents, though, while 92.7 per cent reported being referred to as 'gaijin' at one time or another (a third of them very often), 32.5 per cent were not bothered by it, 17.9 per cent disliked it, 4.1 per cent were made angry by it, 5.7 per cent were saddened and 36.6 per cent marked none of the preceding categories but reported other responses. When this rather surprising finding was aired on the follow-up programme, the survey coordinator commented that the ones who were not bothered by the word were those who had 'given up' (www.debito.org/kume5tvasahibroadcast.html).

A letter was sent to members of ISSHO pointing out that as 'complaint groups' such as the Burakumin, the Ainu and disability support groups routinely made a fuss every time somebody made a gaffe such as Kume's and by so doing had created plenty of 'un-words' (e.g. 'bikko', 'mekura', 'baka-chon') in the Japanese language, the foreign community should follow their example and express its discontent over this incident. Members were urged to call the station and say how much they disliked Kume's comment, which had been made on national TV and infantilized foreigners by suggesting that it was better if they spoke baby-talk Japanese (Aldwinckle 1996). Here too, as in so many other instances, the value of protest by affected groups is recognized, although the chances of success in this instance were not high and in fact no apology was forthcoming.

In this chapter we have examined language protests in relation to ethnic slurs. In the following chapter, we move on to look at the treatment of disability.

# 5

# DISABILITY

A 2001 survey by the Ministry of Health, Labour and Welfare put the number of people with physical disabilities in Japan at around 3.4 million. Another 50,000 intellectually disabled people and 2.18 million people with mental disabilities bring the total to over 6 million (Kusunoki 2002), or around 4.8 per cent of the population. During the 1990s, several things happened which saw the discussion of disability assume a greater than usual degree of prominence. In 1993, the government revised several earlier laws into the Fundamental Law for Disabled Persons. Two years later it announced a seven-year (1996–2002), multi-Ministry National Action Plan for Persons with Disabilities (DPI-JAPAN 1999: 1). Then came the 1996 Law of Promotion of Measures for Human Rights Protection, which encompasses disability within its brief of human rights education. And, of course, the media coverage of the 1998 Winter Paralympics in Nagano focused public attention on the issue as well.

In the same year, the best-selling book *No-one's Perfect* by 23-year-old Ototake Hirotada, born without arms or legs and now famous as both author and newsreader, gave the public a rare first-person account of life in a wheelchair. The book sold 4.4 million copies and has been translated into three languages (Parker 1999). Particularly noteworthy in the Japanese context is its frank rejection of protection of difference. Japanese disability law reflects the European approach, aiming for equality of results by emphasizing special needs over equal rights and mandating quotas, rather than the approach used in the United States, Canada, Great Britain, Australia and New Zealand which aims to provide greater equality of opportunity through laws and measures aimed at ending many forms of discrimination (Heyer 2000: 2).

DPI-JAPAN and other disability advocacy groups in Japan are working towards moving away from the emphasis on protection towards a focus on independence, defended by anti-discrimination provisions. The 1981 United Nations International Year of Disabled Persons (IYDP) mandate of 'full participation and equality' was meant to foster a social model of disability, focusing on equal rights and integration; in fact, however, Japan's disability legislation continues to reflect the medical model. But the IYDP and its equality mandate did generate in Japan 'a new kind of activism that looks to disability movements in the United States as examples of defiant disability pride and rights consciousness. This new generation wants to embrace equal rights and opportunities and move away from the traditional emphasis on special needs' (Heyer 2000: 1).

The discourse of disability worldwide has for some time been the subject of scholarly analysis (see e.g. Corker and French 1999; Marks 1999 and, for textual analysis of the construction of disability on disability websites, Coopman 2000). Linguistic stereotyping and the use of unacceptable terms relating to disability in the public arena have long been a focus of more general attention as well. Academic studies generally take a wider view of the issue, regarding lexical items as encapsulating less easily articulated discourses of discrimination at deeper underlying levels. Much of the general discussion, however, relates specifically to semantics, with particular words and phrases singled out for criticism.

In many countries, considerable effort has gone into establishing policies offering guidelines for how people with disabilities are referred to in the media, focusing on both lexicon and images. Support groups launch active protests against what they consider to be media infractions. In June 2000, for example, SANE Australia, a national group supporting people with intellectual disabilities, complained publicly about the portrayal of schizophrenia in the Jim Carrey film *Me, Myself and Irene*, which the group's executive director described as 'inaccurate, offensive and stigmatising' (Partridge 2000). This group's website (www.sane.org) includes a Stigma Watch section where the public can report inaccurate or inappropriate media coverage of mental illness, providing that the incident appeared in the Australian media (visual and/or print, including advertising), no more than a month previously. Most of the reports currently on the site have to do with the inappropriate use of the word 'schizophrenic'. The approach taken by SANE is reminiscent of that in Japan: 'where a report is verified, those responsible are contacted with an explanation of the harm stigma causes. Responses are posted in the Stigma Files. Serious cases of stigma such as Sony Playstation's game "Twisted Metal Black" in 2001 and haircare company Fudge's

"Schizophrenic" and "Headcase" promotion in 2002 are taken further and may involve national media campaigns'.

In Japan, when students are asked for examples of words they think are discriminatory, terms relating to disability usually head the list. A 1995 survey of 451 undergraduate and graduate students in the Kansai University Sociology Faculty, for instance, found that when respondents were asked to write down words they considered discriminatory the overwhelming majority related to people with disabilities – a total of 1,525 words, compared to 444 about Burakumin and 303 about race (Tamiya 1995: 3). A much smaller group of high-school students participating in a cultural forum at the Peers School in Tokyo gave a similar response, listing words such as 'tsunbo' (deaf), 'bikko' (lame) and 'oshi' (deaf-mute) as those which first sprang to mind when they heard the term 'sabetsu yōgo' (discriminatory language) (Dainikai Bunka Fuoramu 1997: 4). This could be to do with the fact that people with particular kinds of disabilities may be more immediately identifiable than, say, a Burakumin person (who looks just like any other Japanese person) or an ethnic Korean person (who has probably been raised in Japan and speaks Japanese as his/her first language).

The connection between language and discrimination in regard to disability is easy to make. Marks (1999: 138), speaking of English, notes that:

> Language is clearly important in the construction of disability. For example, the vocabulary used to identify impairments is frequently also used as terms of abuse: a person who is not aware of their surroundings and fails to notice something important may be derided as 'blind', a person who fails to listen is 'deaf', while a person who fails to understand something may be taunted with the term 'retard'.

The same is true in Japan, where the secondary meaning of 'mekura' (blind) is 'ignorant', where rubber stamping something without taking time to read the contents properly is called 'mekuraban', where 'mekura meppō ni' means 'in hit and miss fashion', i.e. recklessly, haphazardly and 'kichigai-jimita' indicates 'harebrained', 'crackpot', or 'loony' behaviour. Blindness equates to lack of sense, and mental illness to inability to think carefully.

People with disabilities, of course, face more than purely linguistic discrimination every day. Despite some progress in recent years, full participation in education and employment in Japan remain out of reach regardless of government quotas, as is widely acknowledged in discussion of national human rights issues (see e.g. Tomonaga 1998; DPI-JAPAN 1999), and access to public facilities still has some way to go. But discriminatory language, whether outright verbal abuse or thoughtless stereotyping, has just as much power to exclude as other forms of marginalization and on a deeply personal, stigmatizing level. As with other groups, Japanese disability groups (which include both associations of people with disabilities and associations which work on behalf of people with disabilities, in particular on behalf of children and those with intellectual disabilities) have managed to bring about media compliance with their demands not by being able to build on any strong tradition of civil rights activism but by exploiting the keen desire of the Japanese media to avoid public embarrassment at all costs. International trends have also played a part in both leading to the revision of terminology found in statutes as well as exerting pressure on media to portray people with disabilities fairly.

## The media

The two events which brought most attention to bear on how disability is described in public documents were the IYDP and the 1993 incident involving author Tsutsui Yasutaka. Prior to these, however, the language protest activities of the BLL had paved the way for similar action from disability groups, which led to the inclusion of terms relating to disability in the 'iikaeshū' and 'kinkushū'.

The early 'iikaeshū' in the 1970s included disability-related terms from an early stage. The NTV and TBS broadcasting guidelines for 1973 included small sections on disability. The NET broadcasting guidelines the same year did not, being mainly Burakumin-oriented, but by the following year the list had grown considerably and included a much larger list of terms than did NTV and TBS. It was now divided into sections classified as a) alternatives to words to be avoided in broadcasting, b) slang and c) words which can give offence. Within the first of these sections were a further three subdivisions, into 'sabetsu yōgo' (discriminatory language), 'shokugyō o iyashimu kotoba' (demeaning terms for occupations) and 'keibetsu no kotoba' (contemptuous words). Those relating to disability fell within the third of these subsections. The words and their prescribed alternatives are set out in Table 5.1.

What is interesting here is that mentioning the names of physical conditions such as epilepsy and meningitis is considered on a par

102

*Table 5.1* Proscribed words

| Not to be used | Substitute |
|---|---|
| izari (cripple) | ryōashi no fujiyū na hito (person without the use of both legs) |
| oshi (deaf-mute) | kuchi no fujiyū na hito (person without the use of his/her mouth) |
| katateochi (unfair, lit: one-armed) | fukōhei (unfair) |
| katawa, fugusha (cripple) | shintai shōgaisha (person with a physical disability) |
| gachame, ronpari (squint) | shashi (strabismus) |
| kijirushi (crackpot) | seishinshōgaishi (person with an |
| kichigai (crazy – don't use at all) | intellectual disability) |
| koke (fool) | |
| tenkan (epilepsy) | |
| nōmakuen (meningitis) | |
| hakuchi (idiot) | |
| -kichi, -kichigai (mad about-) | -mania |
| kichigai o nobanashi ni (let the nuts take care of themselves) | absolutely not to be used |
| kichigai ni hamono (giving a knife to a madman) | absolutely not to be used |
| kyōki no sata (a state of madness) | try not to use |
| tensai to kyōjin wa kami hitoe (genius is only one remove from insanity) | try not to use |
| chinba, bikko (cripple) | ashi no fujiyū na hito (person without the full use of his/her leg(s)) |
| tsunbo (deaf) | rōsha (deaf person) |
| tsunbo sajiki (upper gallery) | sogai sareru basho (a distant place), kikoenai tokoro (place where you can't hear things properly) |
| domori (stutter) | gengoshōgaisha (person with a speech disability) |
| mitsukuchi (hare lip) | toshin (hare lip) |
| mekura, domekura (blind) | me no fujiyū na hito (person without the use of his/her eyes), mōmoku no hito, mōjin (blind person) |

*Table 5.1* cont'd

| Not to be used | Substitute |
| --- | --- |
| mekurauchi (hitting blindly) | |
| mekurajima (dark blue cotton cloth) mekura hebi no ojizu (fools rush in where angels fear to tread) mekura meppō (reckless) | avoid where possible |
| mekuraban (rubber stamp, lit: using one's seal without looking) | roku ni minai de han o osu (stamp one's seal without looking properly) |
| mekkachi (one-eyed) | katame no fujiyū no hito (person without the use of one eye), dokugan, sekigan |
| raibyō (leprosy) | Hansenbyō (Hansen's disease) |

*Source*: Yōgo to Sabetsu o kangaeru Shimpojiumu Jikkō Iinkai (1989: 291–6).

with calling someone crazy or an idiot and is not to be done on air, thus depriving people with epilepsy of an avenue for raising public awareness of the condition; it is treated in this list as being a term of stigma equivalent to slang references to mental disability. The allegorical use of madness in proverbs and clichés is also to be avoided. The words and expressions singled out for avoidance or replacement are those which focus attention on the disability rather than the person; which stigmatize those with the disability by metaphorically relating some socially unacceptable behaviour to it; or which stereotype people with disabilities in some way, usually by showing them as helpless or pitiful (an image which Ototake's book has single-handedly done much to overturn).

Media self-censorship on the subject of disability was thus well in place by 1980 and was further reinforced in 1981 during the IYDP when publishing and broadcasting circles pledged vigilance in eradicating the use of discriminatory terms. The World Programme of Action concerning Disabled Persons, adopted by the United Nations General Assembly in late 1982 as an outcome of the IYDP, stressed the importance of the media in achieving the desired outcome of a change in social attitudes towards disability:

Guidelines should be developed in consultation with organizations of disabled persons to encourage the news media to give a sensitive and accurate portrayal of, as well as fair

representation of and reporting on, disabilities and disabled
persons in radio, television, film, photography and print.
(United Nations 1982: 7)

Continuing external expectations of this type combined with ongoing domestic embarrassment whenever a breach occurred as disability support groups found their voices encouraged compliance with
the use of neutral language. Apart from in-house collections, general
guidelines given to journalists in editions of the *Kisha Handobukku*
today include advice about words to be avoided, not as detailed as
in the table above but covering the major bases. The 1999 edition,
for example, carries a collection of words listed as 'sabetsugo'
(discriminatory language) or 'fukai yōgo' (unpleasant terminology)
which includes items related to physical and mental disabilities, as
above (Kyōdō Tsūshinsha 1999: 82).

Of the words listed, it is probably 'kichigai' which has attracted the
most complaint, particularly because of its problematic association
with other activities, in a parallel with the English 'mad' (e.g. 'sports-
mad'). 'Mekura' also became a focus of censure because of its secondary meaning of 'ignorance'; so, by association, did those words in
which 'mekura' occurred as a component, for example, 'mekuraban'
(signing a paper without reading the contents), 'mekurakabe' (a blind
wall), even 'mekurajima' (a dark blue cotton cloth). 'Tsunbo sajiki',
meaning 'upper gallery', carried the double meaning of being utterly
ignored, intimating that deaf people ('tsunbo') merited no attention.

The substitute terms resemble those adopted in other countries,
where expressions such as 'person with a disability' replaced 'the
disabled'. The Australian Government's Office of Disability, for
example, advised that the term 'person with a disability' was to be
preferred to 'the disabled' or 'disabled persons' because 'it recognizes
that a disability is only one characteristic of an individual and does
not imply any generalized lack of ability'. The government's guide to
dealing with specific disabilities (Office of Government Information
and Advertising 1997) paralleled practice in Japan: 'cripple', for
instance, should be replaced either by the non-specific 'person with
a disability' or the name of the specific disability (e.g. 'paraplegic';
'deaf-mute' became 'deaf/hearing-impaired/speech-impaired').
'Crazy/insane/dull-witted' was replaced by 'person with a psychiatric
disability'. So too in Japan: 'hakuchi' (imbecility) has now become
'chiteki shōgai' (intellectual disability) in the laws and 'kichigai'
(crazy) has been replaced by 'seishin shōgaisha' (person with a
mental disability).

These revisions of terminology, while on the surface unexceptional and clearly taken up dutifully by the mass media and the makers of computer dictionaries, have not been unmarked by controversy along the way. At times, protests have been lodged against what is seen as unacceptable censorship, as in the 1983 case of an unsuccessful candidate in the Lower House election when NHK cut a section of his broadcast of his political opinions because it contained two words, 'mekanchi' and 'chinba' (lame), which the broadcaster deemed discriminatory. The candidate's party brought a lawsuit for 2 million yen in damages against NHK and the state, claiming that the arbitrary removal of the words from the broadcast constituted a violation of the Public Office Election Law. The court upheld this view: although the words in question were discriminatory, the candidate had merely been quoting someone else. NHK was ordered to pay 600,000 yen in damages for the infringement (Takagi 1999: 133).

Complaints continue from time to time. In 1999, for example, high-profile academic and social commentator Takeshi Yōrō criticized the media's adoption of self-censorship. Discussing what he sees as the exclusionary nature of the Japanese definition of humanity, Yōrō wrote:

Thanks to efforts to root out 'discriminatory language', it has become almost impossible to talk about such things. Those leading the charge against discriminatory language, incidentally, are not groups that are discriminated against but the media, the self-appointed arbiters of society! Since discussion is all but taboo, people cannot be expected to understand what the problem is. The unspoken definition of humanity is at the root of socially contentious issues.

(Yōrō 1999: 6)

Yōrō is wrong: disability groups have been active in protesting since the 1970s, and that is what led to change on the part of the media. In 1974, for example, the use of the word 'kichigai' (mad) to characterize rowdy antisocial behaviour in a broadcast of *The Lordless Retainers of Arano* led the Osaka Association of Families of People with Intellectual Disabilities to complain to Mainichi Broadcasting, on the grounds that medical evidence showed that exposure to such words had deleterious effects on patients and their families (Takagi 1999: 110–11). This was far from an isolated incident (see Takagi 1999 for more). Subtitlers of films as a result became subject to restrictions on terminology. On one occasion the traditional New York motorist's cry of 'whatsa matta, you deaf?' was rendered in Japanese as 'whassa matta, you unable to hear?' And in the 1970s Japanese version of *Monty Python's Flying Circus*, John Cleese's Ministry of Silly Walks was cut for fear of protests from disability support groups (Bailey 1998: 1–2).

Complaints such as Yōrō's illustrate that on occasion an over-focus on language change can deflect attention from deficiencies in public policy. The problems faced by people with disabilities are there to be seen. To say that they cannot be discussed because of media monitoring of language ignores the possibility of conducting the debate in non-offensive terms, fobs off responsibility for social policy on to the media, and locates the cause of lack of action in inclusive language rather than in entrenched government attitudes.

## Laws and statutes

Terminology revision in laws and statutes began with a city councillor with a disability in Shinano in Nagano Prefecture (the same prefecture which later hosted the Winter Paralympics), who in late 1980 suggested that the statutes be rewritten to achieve greater consonance with the welfare era. Until that time, 'fugu', 'haishitsu', 'tsunbo', 'mekura', 'oshi' and other such words had routinely been used. As a result, the city council removed the words 'fugu haishitsusha' (the crippled and deformed) from its documents and called for the revision of prefectural and national laws and statutes as well. This fledgling movement was spurred along the following year by the IYDP, during which the terminology issue was taken up at national government level. 'Fugu/haishitsusha' was discovered to occur in ordinances at all levels of government, and in a total of 11 laws, including the Self-Defence Forces Law Enforcement Ordinance. The Ministry of Health and Welfare revised a total of 9 laws, including the Medical Practitioners Law, the Dental Practitioners Law and the Public-Health Nurses, Midwives and Nurses Law, replacing 'fugu' and 'haishitsu' with the more neutral 'shōgai' (disability), and 'mekura', 'tsunbo' and 'oshi' with 'me ga mienai mono', 'mimi ga kikoenai mono' and 'kuchi ga kikoenai mono' (a person whose eyes/ears/mouth don't/doesn't see/hear/work) respectively (Takagi 1999: 130–1). Clearly the IYDP was a motivating factor both in the media (to a certain extent) and government arenas; without that international impetus, change may have been slower in coming.

As with the media, changes to legal terminology have not always been undisputed. Public perceptions of disability often derive from how that term is defined. The medical model, to which as we have seen Japan subscribes, constructs disability in terms of individual flaws which prevent people from living a 'normal' life and require medical intervention or rehabilitation. The social model, on the other hand, defines disability in terms of culture and social environment, siting the difficulty not with the person involved but with the expectations of the social milieu within which he or she must operate. Western activists developed social model definitions in reaction to the medical model in the 1970s, as exemplified by the Union of the Physically Impaired Against Segregation (UPIAS) in Britain. The UPIAS defined the lack of or defective functioning of some part of the body as impairment, and disability as 'the disadvantage or restriction of activity caused by a contemporary social organisation which takes no or little account of people who have physical impairments and thus excludes them from participation in the mainstream of social activities' (UPIAS 1976, cited in Swain and Cameron 1999: 69).

'Shōgaisha' (disabled person) being the official term in the revised statutes, government organs such as the Ministry of Justice, the Ministry of Health, Labour and Welfare and the Prime Minister's Office use it freely in committee names, surveys, publications and websites. The term has been criticized, however, by Japanese advocates of the social model, who feel that it focuses on the notion of damaged individuals rather than social barriers to participation. The IYDP was called in Japanese 'kokusai shōgaisha nen'. NHK chief director Nohara Masao, writing in 1982 about the role of the media in the IYDP, took issue with the term 'shōgai', which means a hindrance or handicap, subjecting it to a character-based linguistic analysis. The label exacerbated individual differences between people which were no more than a matter of degree, he argued; differences between people were just that, differences, conditions specific to individuals, and not disabilities. The character 'gai' (harm, injury, damage, obstruction) used to write the second half of the word invariably occurs in words with a less than salubrious meaning, such as 'kōgai' (pollution), 'saigai' (disaster), 'satsugai' (murder), 'hakugai' (oppression), 'heigai' (vice) and 'kagai' (violence). Where it occurs as the first character in a word, it means 'harmful': 'gaichū' (vermin, harmful insects), 'gaichō' (injurious birds), 'gai-i' (ill will). Why, Nohara asked, should a character with such a meaning be used in the words '(shō)gaisha' (disabled person) or '(shō)gaiji' (disabled child)? Its continued use during the United Nations Decade of Disabled Persons (1983–1992) which was to follow the IYDP would entrench the binary opposition between those with 'gai' and those with 'health'; as a result, the word 'shōgaisha' itself would become a discriminatory term (Nohara 1982: 40–1).

Namase (1994: 89) agrees: while a 'shōgai' is no more than one of an individual's distinguishing features, a 'shōgaisha' is a social construct, a recipient of discrimination created by the social environment and attitudes. In this he echoes the United Nations' viewpoint: 'A major lesson of the Year was that the image of persons with disabilities depends to an important extent on social attitudes; these were a major barrier to the realization of the goal of full participation and equality in society by persons with disabilities' (United Nations 2000). By its encapsulation of this attitudinal dimension, the term 'shōgaisha' remains problematic for some, to the extent that one website on disability welfare badges its entrance level with an implicit apology for using the word 'shōgai', explaining that it does so only because that is the present legal terminology (Shōgai Fukushi).

The nature of written Japanese is a factor in decisions about terminology: the conciseness afforded by the use of characters versus the tedium of spelling the whole thing out in longer terms. Members of the Osaka Society for Visually Impaired People, for example, chose not to use the word 'mō' because if it were written with a character it could be read 'mekura'; they therefore decided to use the term 'shiryoku shōgaisha' (people with a visual disability). They changed their minds, however, after discovering that when the term 'mōrōjin hōmu' (a home for blind elderly people) was changed to 'shiryoku ni shōgai o ukete iru rōjin hōmu', it became too unwieldy (Yōgo to Sabetsu o kangaeru Shimpojiumu Jikkō Iinkai 1989: 197). Likewise, when deaf people refer to themselves in TV programmes they use the short word 'rōsha' rather than the longer euphemisms (Valentine 2001: 710).

With 'shōgaisha', characters offer two alternative possibilities, one of which extends the length of the word by just one syllable and another which keeps it much the same. In the first, the prefix 'hi' (recipient) might be added to indicate that a person is the recipient of a disability enforced on him/her by society, as happened with Burakumin: instead of 'Burakumin', the officially sanctioned term became 'hisabetsu burakumin' (discriminated-against Burakumin). The other is to change the disputed 'gai' character in the middle for another character pronounced the same but meaning 'barrier', to indicate that the person faces obstacles put in their way by society rather than that they are in some way damaged. Or the 'gai' part can just be written in the phonetic hiragana script, thus removing the visual reference to 'harm'. Shiki City in Saitama Prefecture changed to this way of writing the word in its documentation in 2001 (Channel 2 discussion thread 2001). The mayor of Sapporo city in Hokkaido announced the same change to council documentation there in 2003 (*Asahi Shimbun* 2003).

The Channel 2 website, as we saw in Chapter 2, is a source of contention over the kinds of language some of its users employ to abuse minority groups. People with disabilities are by no means exempt. One thread, entitled 'konna shōgaisha wa iya da' (I hate these people with disabilities),[1] carries messages offering an assassination service for people who would like to see people with disabilities killed; another suggests that anyone who gives birth to a disabled child should give it to a Chinese person, who would cook and eat it; another doesn't like people with disabilities who breathe in oxygen and exhale carbon dioxide; yet another doesn't like 'shōgaisha' who are ungrateful, who could have done things for themselves instead of asking others, and who make a fuss about their rights and care nothing for their obligations. The list goes on, and that is only one of the archived threads.

Contributors to the Channel 2 discussion thread on how to write 'shōgaisha' talked about other possibilities for reshaping this word, suggesting a different character also meaning 'barrier' and pronounced 'gai'. Interspersed with the useful discussion were the usual Channel 2 comments from non-sympathizers, to the effect that the middle character could be 'gai' (corpse) or that the word 'katawa' (cripple) would do. One interesting point, though, in what became quite a lengthy discussion was that if the purpose of changing the written representation of the word was to improve the image of people with disabilities, just fiddling with terminology would not be enough to achieve that aim, as the word 'shōgaisha' itself must have become a discriminatory term if it needed to be replaced.

It is true that carefully constructed terms intended to be neutral have a limited life span before they themselves take on the discriminatory overtones of the terms they replaced. This may happen more slowly in the disability sphere than elsewhere, simply because the redefinitions of disability are so long and sometimes clumsy (the lengthy 'ashi ga fujiyū na hito' instead of the short, sharp and nasty 'bikko', for example). As Valentine (1998: 7.4) observes,

Long clumsy euphemisms are restricted in usage. They thereby retain their value as euphemisms for the experts or official bodies that use them: their coating is used up less rapidly. Extended euphemisms can last for an extended period: a euphemism that is inflated in size is less subject to the inflationary process that requires perpetual replacement. The inflation has already gone into the length of the expression, and so does not give rise to such frequent substitution.

It remains to be seen whether 'shōgaisha' will be replaced with something else. Given the government propensity regarding language to stick with something once decided, however, that may not happen for some time at the national level of laws and statutes. Meanwhile, as we have seen, some change is taking place in the practices at the level of local municipalities; grassroots action often precedes top-down policy in Japan. A longer euphemism already in use is 'karada no fujiyū na kata' (person with a physical disability), which lacks the punch of the more concise 'shōgaisha'.

The IYDP coincided with a worldwide movement on the part of people with disabilities to form alliances which would work to highlight existing stigmatization and discrimination. In Japan, with its emphasis on difference and protection, this struggle has been more torturous than in those countries which have followed the United States' approach. The Disability Policy Research Group called for anti-discrimination legislation to be included in the revision of disability laws scheduled for 2000, but as yet no legal barriers to discrimination are in place. The lack of a strong civil rights tradition like that in the Unites States, where African-Americans and women blazed the way, underpins the Japanese legislation's emphasis on protection rather than rights. Activists, however, are now increasingly attempting to politicize the movement by using the language of civil rights and anti-discrimination to frame their demands (Heyer 2000: 7).

While the content of laws in Japan may continue to reflect the protection approach, then, at least some progress has been made in the area of language. Just as protectionism functions to separate, so too does language which labels people as different or inferior, and the revision of legal terminology in response to the IYDP recognized this. Further sporadic revision has occurred since then: when the legal definition of a disabled person was expanded to include people with mental disabilities in 1993, for example, the term 'shintai shōgaisha' (physically disabled person), which had been used to refer to people with disabilities of every kind in the 1970 Physically Disabled People's Fundamental Law, was replaced with the broader 'shōgaisha' to reflect the new definition (Heyer 2000: 7). These changes, however, are ad hoc, and do not represent an across-the-board commitment to equality of representation and opportunity on the part of the government as yet.

## The Tsutsui Yasutaka incident

As we saw in Chapter 2, literature has provided fertile ground for arguments over language, as have some of the performing arts, with exponents of the popular narrative art *rakugo* complaining that their stories, which often contain words such as 'tsunbo' or 'mekura', have been seriously disadvantaged following the restrictions on media terminology (Morioka 1990: 276–7). The best-known case of a protest relating to literature is what is known as the Tsutsui Yasutaka incident mentioned in Chapter 2. To recap: in 1993, the JEA protested against the inclusion in a school textbook of a short story by Tsutsui, a prominent writer, which they believed encouraged discrimination against people with epilepsy (see Namase 1994: 97–100). Tsutsui's publisher, Kadokawa, supported him, but the author was outraged at what he termed unacceptable 'language hunts' and announced that he would give up writing in protest, which he did for several years. The incident provoked an impassioned debate between human rights activists on the one hand and anti-censorship advocates on the other. A multitude of TV interviews, magazine articles and books (e.g. Oyama 1994; Shiomi 1994 and Gekkan 'Tsukuru' Henshūbu 1995) covered the subject.

Fellow writer Sono Ayako spoke out on Tsutsui's behalf, likening attempts to suppress literary freedom in this way to the prewar suppression of freedom of speech, and worse, freedom of thought. Sono indicated that 'a minority of discreet editors who themselves are trying to fight against suppression' had supported her, suggesting that not all sectors of the publishing industry were wholeheartedly behind the banning of discriminatory terms. The media, in her view, were too easily cowed: the tactics of the support groups themselves, in demanding apologies and in some cases financial compensation, constituted harassment and attempts to suppress freedom of speech, and yet they went virtually unopposed. To insist on rigid guidelines in acceptable language use did nothing to inculcate a true spirit of respect towards those delineated by such terms, she argued; indeed, the irritation of repression was perhaps likely to produce just the opposite effect (Sono 1993). In this she was probably quite correct, and yet one must question values which put freedom of speech above the courtesy of inclusion. Literature has always been seen by some, however, as a special case, the writer's muse being deemed sacrosanct and therefore exempt from social sanctions of this sort.

Equally respected writer and Nobel Prize winner Oe Kenzaburō, who has a son with an intellectual disability, disagreed with Sono. Was it really true that Tsutsui could no longer write if he couldn't use certain words, he asked? Oe himself opposed the mechanical replacement of contested terms with others, believing that it did nothing to address the realities of discrimination and could hand a weapon to those bent on discriminating. But Tsutsui's story gave inaccurate and insufficient information about epilepsy and was not worthy of being included in a textbook as an example of his work. Much better for him to write carefully than to isolate himself by not writing (Oe 1994: 13).

Tamiya's 1995 survey, mentioned above, also questioned students on their perceptions of the Tsutsui incident. The results showed that the nature of the controversy was imperfectly understood: many respondents believed the fuss had been caused by the use of the word 'tenkan' (epilepsy) itself, which was not the case. What had been at issue for the JEA had been the manner in which people with epilepsy had been portrayed rather than the use of the name of the condition itself. This misinterpretation indicated that while social awareness of 'sabetsugo' (discriminatory language) was high, the concept of 'sabetsu hyōgen' (stereotyping through description rather than by naming) was less well-understood (Tamiya 1995: 56). The robot police who checked the brain waves of drivers in Tsutsui's short story were under orders to send anyone in whom certain patterns were detected to hospital, in order to prevent the presumed danger of people with epilepsy driving. The implication that epilepsy prevented people from leading normal lives and merited segregation in hospitals was seen as perpetuating the old prejudice against those with this condition. Many students, however, missed this distinction entirely and thought both that the word 'epilepsy' itself had been used and that the JEA had been over-sensitive in its reaction, indicating that the principles behind inclusive language theory had yet to penetrate to any significant extent in at least this section of society.

The whole issue of literary freedom versus the sensitivities of minorities was thrust into the public spotlight by the incident, which brought to the surface a previously unarticulated (or at least publicly unarticulated) discontent over what were perceived as unreasonable restrictions on freedom of speech. We saw in Chapter 2 that by 1995 the Japan PEN Club was sufficiently concerned by the growing perception of increased policing of language that it surveyed its members for their experiences, publishing the findings in a special volume devoted to the issue. Just under 80 per cent of those who responded reported experiencing some form of editorial or other intervention relating to acceptability of language, most typically in the context of newspapers, magazines and books but occasionally also in broadcasts. In almost half of these cases, the terms involved had been seen as making discriminatory references to physical or mental characteristics (see Nihon PEN Kurabu 1995 and Gottlieb 1998).

Meanwhile, 12 years later, the JEA continues to maintain a comprehensive archive of documents relating to the Tsutsui incident on its website at www.synapse.ne.jp/jepnet/KOKUGO/kyoukasyo.html, with a link to a detailed chronology of developments, including correspondence, under the heading 'Particulars of the Kadokawa Textbook Epilepsy Discrimination Problem'. The main page contains the text of an urgent announcement in the JEA newsletter of the beginning of a campaign of protest against the publisher, other related excerpts from the newsletter, and a collection of correspondence between the JEA, Tsutsui and the publisher Kadokawa detailing the Association's concerns and the other side's responses. Clearly the language and stereotyping issues embodied by the incident remain a major concern for the Association, which has thus kept information available on the internet to keep the issue alive.

## Manga and disability

Disability activists have often targeted the immensely popular Japanese *manga* (cartoon). 'They are quick to identify material they consider offensive, and their pressure on store owners and distributors can instantly ruin the sales of a magazine or book' (Schodt 1983: 130). Protests have centred both on actual language use and on stereotyping. A 1998 book, *Manga no Naka no Shōgaisha-tachi* (*Images of People with Disabilities in Comics*), catalogues *manga* which portray people who are deaf or have other disabilities; its author, Akira Nagai, is himself deaf. While many portrayals are accurate, Nagai notes, some are biased or misleading, reflecting commonly-held views at the time they were written. A common assumption in *manga* of the 1950s and 1960s, for example, was that people who could not speak could not communicate, with gangs attempting to silence people who might threaten their security by robbing them in some way of their voice. This nexus between voice suppression (whether by tongue removal, medication or other means) and secret-keeping persisted into the 1970s and 1980s. Words such as 'tsunbo' were bandied about disparagingly in contexts such as 'who else would look twice at a tsunbo woman like you?'; a woman's inability to make a sound was seen as convenient for rapists. Those few people in wheelchairs who appeared in *manga* were apt to be portrayed as objects of pity, rescued by the 'kindness' of their partners and bewailing the 'burden' (futan) they represented to others, rather than as people with equal rights with the able-bodied. Given the enormous popularity of *manga*, the power of these images should not be underestimated.

But *manga* have been used to break down stereotypes as well. Yamamoto Osamu dealt with deafness in a positive way in *Donguri no Ie (Donguri's House)* and other *manga*. Through his own study of sign language, Yamamoto gradually became aware of the discrimination which deaf people routinely encounter, and the realization led him to incorporate these themes in his *manga*. *Donguri no Ie* was awarded a prize by the Japan Manga Association in 1995 and later became an 'anime' (animated) film. Producing such a work was not easy: such was the *manga* world's fear of criticism for using discriminatory language by then that even writing about 'shōgaisha mondai' (the problem of the disabled) was viewed as taboo. Nevertheless, Yamamoto subscribes to the social model, believing that the so-called 'problem of the disabled' lies not with people with disabilities themselves but with the way society reacts to them (*Asahi Shimbun* 1997), and his work is an effort to address this.

A second work to tackle the issue of discrimination head-on is Kobayashi Yoshinori's *Gōmanizumu Sengen: Sabetsuron Supesharu (A Declaration of Arrogant-ism: Discrimination Special* 1995), a collection of pieces which make up a volume in a *manga* series published by Kobayashi dealing in an outspoken manner with often controversial issues. Images strongly influence cultural constructions of disability everywhere, as is well documented (e.g. Thomson 1997). As *manga*, many of which are written for adults, account for well over half of all magazines published in Japan, highly visible authors of this genre have particular potential to sway their readers' perceptions of disability. Positive expansion of the debate into *manga* is therefore greatly to be desired as a step along the way to changing social attitudes.

We have seen in this chapter that organized domestic pressure from disability groups combined with the significant external influence of the IYDP and subsequent United Nations activities contributed to the shift in the language used to discuss disability in Japan. Language constructs social practice as much as it reflects it, in a two-way process which informs both perceptions and their inevitable outcomes. Japan's approach to disability rights has never been as proactive or as progressive as its activists might wish. As long as the language issue is kept in the public eye, however, by whatever means, people will be asked to rethink their assumptions and consider the implications of the words they carelessly use. A deeper understanding of how language shapes attitudes and subsequent practice therefore contributes to community awareness of disability issues in Japan as elsewhere in a particularly powerful and personal way. Changes to public policy will come from the work of lobby groups, not from changes in the language of public documents, but the social milieu into which those policy changes eventually emerge can only have benefited from the inclusive language debate.

# 6

# GENDER

Language relating to women, like that relating to people with disabilities, came under scrutiny both as the result of international movements and the activities of the BLL. Social changes resulting from the guaranteed equality of men and women in the postwar Constitution, the women's liberation movement overseas in the 1960s and the growth of its Japanese counterpart in the 1970s, the 1985 United Nations Convention on the Elimination of All Forms of Discrimination against Women, and, in Japan, the passing of the Equal Employment Opportunity Law (EEOL) in 1986 all contributed. The EEOL, revised in 1997 to place greater emphasis on the responsibilities of employers, was particularly influential: protests about discriminatory terms and references to women grew alongside their increasing participation in employment.

Ingrained community attitudes, however, usually fail to keep pace with social changes brought about by government, and so many of the words disputed by feminists, such as 'mibōjin' (widow, lit. not yet dead person) and 'kanai' (my wife, lit. inside my house), remain in use. Japan is very much a case of language change not having caught up with social change, except at a very superficial level, in the area of gender. While social change in the last 30 years has certainly advanced the cause of gender equality, not least because of the declining birth rate in the 1990s, older structures of discrimination remain evident in the lexicon. Women's groups have carried out protests from time to time, as we shall see, but these have by and large lacked the force and degree of determination – and therefore power to bring about compliance – of those of the BLL. While the actual language practice of the media towards women may have altered slightly and small gains have been made in the 'iikaeshū', sexism remains entrenched at a much deeper level in the language used to speak of women in general.

'Women experience linguistic discrimination in two ways: in the way they are taught to use language, and in the way general language use treats them. Both tend . . . to relegate women to certain subservient functions: that of sex object, or servant' (Lakoff 1975: 4). Lakoff was speaking of English, but the same is true of Japan, as we shall see in this chapter. In Lakoff's view, linguistic change follows from social change, rather than the other way round. This idea is contested by Valian (1981: 74–9), who argues that 'social change is not sufficient to guarantee linguistic change. But even if it is insufficient, it could still be necessary'. She cites the case of the early years of the women's movement as an example of linguistic change preceding social change, when the way in which feminists spoke influenced a change in other people's speech habits well before changes to education or employment conditions. In Japan, where the women's movement surfaced later than in the United States, the two went more or less hand in hand: the Equal Employment Opportunity Law was passed at the same time that women's groups were actively complaining about terms used to refer to them.

In a general philosophical meditation on sexist language, Shute (1981: 25) speaks of:

> the rather simple-minded claim that people cannot help to eliminate sexism merely by 'talk,' by replacing 'terms' with other 'terms,' but only by *actions*. Such a claim embodies a failure to distinguish between words qua words and words qua used by speakers of the language. Words qua words are powerless to effect any change in the world, but the use of words is a human activity with nonlinguistic effects in the world. Seen from this latter aspect, the use of words (terms) can have the same effect as activities (and their non-linguistic effects) such as paying employees on the basis of sex rather than ability.

And further, 'sexist language . . . is thus a *part of* sexism in any society where sexism exists; it constitutes an instance of sexism . . . The upshot of this is that elimination of sexist language is necessary for eliminating sexism in any society' (Shute 1981: 31). The discrimination, in other words, lies in the use of the words rather than the words themselves. If it is the use of terms that discriminates, then, the decision not to use them can presumably help to dispel discrimination.

The success or otherwise of attempts to change gender bias in language depends very much on the social context surrounding the language reform. 'When language reform occurs within the context of a larger socio-political initiative whose primary goal is the eradication of sexist practices (e.g. employment equity programmes), it is more likely to succeed. By contrast, when language reform occurs within the context of a speech community that embraces sexist values and attitudes, it is less likely to succeed' (Ehrlich and King 1998: 165). In Japan, as we saw in Chapter 1, the media crackdown on language targeting particular groups occurred out of fear of public embarrassment through being exposed to public complaint rather than from any considered attempt to address the underlying discrimination and to reflect that in media language use. The early stages of the women's movement itself did not focus on language; this came quite late, by comparison with the early feminist protests over linguistic practice in English-speaking countries, partly because of a failure to see the connection between language and social oppression and partly because 'Japanese women tend to work within patriarchal society, rather than work to destroy it . . . language, which reproduces patriarchal society, was hardly mentioned in the course of women's liberation' (Abe 1995).

This can be seen by the relative paucity of changes made to gender-related expressions in the press. The early 'iikaeshū' contained only scant reference to women; their emphasis was on words relating to Burakumin, occupation ( = by extension, in many cases though not all, Burakumin) and disability, reflecting the sections of the community from which the most vehement protests had been received. What few gender-related examples were given at the beginning of the 1970s were limited to 'onnakodomo', 'jochū' (maid) and 'jokō' (factory girl) (on the grounds of occupation), and 'mekake' (mistress). 'Jochū' and 'jokō' were the only gender-related terms to figure in both the 1973 TBS list and NTV list. In the 1974 NET guidelines, several expressions are listed in the category of 'words that might upset people' rather than in the 'words which relate to human rights' or 'slang' categories: they include 'onnakodomo', 'yome ni yaru' (to marry one's daughter off), and 'musume o katazukeru' (to marry one's daughter off). Although this is an 'iikaeshū' (list of substitute terms) and not a 'kinkushū' (list of forbidden terms, with no substitutes suggested), no alternatives are given for these expressions: they are simply marked 'narubeku tsukawanai' (try not to use them at all). And so on through the early lists of other companies (see Yōgo to Sabetsu o kangaeru Shinpojiumu Jikkō Iinkai 1989 for a collection).

## Government takes the lead

Government organs early on took a more proactive line. During the 1980s, thanks in large part to the rewording of documents relating to people with disabilities and also to the larger social debate relating to the status of women both in Japan and internationally, some areas of government began to examine their documentation to see whether inappropriate terminology relating to women might be removed. The International Convention on the Elimination of All Forms of Discrimination Against Women (1981), which Japan ratified in 1985, stipulates in Article 5 that 'States Parties shall take all appropriate measures . . . to modify the social and cultural patterns of conduct of men and women, with a view to achieving the elimination of prejudices and customary and all other practices which are based on the idea of the inferiority or the superiority of either of the sexes of on stereotyped roles for men and women'. In 1984, the Kanagawa prefectural government instituted the Kanagawa Women's Plan, predicated on improving expressions and content relating to women in prefectural publications, in particular with reference to gender-determined divisions of labour. Each prefectural organization was requested to examine its publications in order to detect and remove traditional gender-role stereotypes and views of male-female relations (particularly in the family context) which were remnants of the patriarchal feudal system and words which expressed bias or contempt towards women. The overall aim was to revise the belief that women's lives were played out inside the house and family only, and to encourage participation by men in those domains as well. Women were to be portrayed as having a fundamental right to work. Some of the expressions removed were: 'shokuba no hana' ('office flower', a term used to denote young, decorative female employees who performed only the lightest of office duties and whose term of employment was short); 'ikka no daikakubashira wa yahari chichi oya' (the most important member of a family is the father); 'fukei-shijo' (fathers and brothers, children and women); 'onna no kusatta yō ni' (like a rotten woman); and expressions such as 'josei wa judōteki' (women are passive) which stereotyped women's characteristics. The word 'fujin' (lady, with a strong overtone of 'married woman') was also replaced in many government contexts with the more neutral 'josei' (woman) (Takagi 1999: 145–8), just as in the West the women's movement campaigned to have 'lady' replaced with 'woman'. Many national and prefectural government offices changed their names to remove this word; in 1994, for example, the 'fujin mondai tantōshitsu' (Office in charge of Women's Issues) set up in the Prime Minister's Office in 1975 was renamed the 'danjo byōdō sankashitsu' (Office for Gender Equality). However, Saitama Prefecture retains its 'Kokuritsu Fujin Kyōiku Kaikan' (National Women's Education Centre); several offices also contain the word 'fujin' in their title. It makes announcements like 'Fujin mondai kōza de josei puran o gakushū suru' (we will study the Plan for Women at the women's issues lectures), mixing the two words in one sentence (Ueno 1998: 95).

The 1996 Hyogo Prefectural Women's Centre *Hyōgen Handobukku* (*Handbook of Expression*) is an example of a local government publication on the approach to language which should inform prefectural publications. It carried a four-page article on language and gender discrimination which commented on the enduring stereotypes: that men are better than women and so occupy positions of control, that the rules for gender roles are fundamentally different (men outside, women inside; men in command, women subordinate), and that women are to be treated as sex objects. Examples were given of language about women and work which indicated that women were inferior to men, including the 'onnadatera ni' contested by Endō as we saw in Chapter 2, and of language which objectified women in a sexual way. Phrases encapsulating fossilized gender roles which take no account of individual differences between people were also to be avoided (e.g.: 'onna no kuse ni/otoko no kuse ni', onna rashii/ otoko rashii').

The government's Plan for Gender Equality 2000 was designed to meet the Platform for Action which resulted from the United Nations Fourth World Conference (FWCW) on Women in Beijing in 1995. The Platform contained a section on women and the media, which suggested *inter alia* that in order to prevent media stereotyping of women governments should 'encourage the media to refrain from presenting women as inferior beings and exploiting them as sexual objects and commodities, rather than presenting them as creative human beings, key actors and contributors to and beneficiaries of the process of development' and, in circular fashion, 'promote the concept that the sexist stereotypes displayed in the media are gender discriminatory, degrading in nature and offensive'. The mass media and advertising organizations, for their part, were to 'develop, consistent with freedom of expression, professional guidelines and codes of conduct and other forms of self-regulation to promote the presentation of non-stereotyped images of women' (FWCW n.d.).

As a flow-on from the Beijing Conference and following the passing of the Basic Law for a Gender-equal Society in 1999, the government drew up a document (*Plan for Gender Equality 2000: The National Plan of Action for Promotion of a Gender-equal Society by the Year 2000*)[1] which contained a section to the effect that it would promote gender-free expressions in official releases and publications of official organizations in the following ways. The basic direction informing any measures was:

> In order to project diverse images of women and men throughout society, not limiting those images to gender-based stereotypes, the Government and other official organizations should take the lead in formulating guidelines on methods for portraying gender in publications, etc. Promotional efforts must also be made so that independent efforts even by the private media will be made in line with the efforts of official organizations.

As concrete measures, the government would:

- formulate guidelines on official releases and publications;
- formulate guidelines, from the perspective of gender equality, that must be observed in the official releases and publications of official organizations, and positively project diverse images of women and men, not limiting those images to gender-based stereotypes;
- inform the private sector of the guidelines;
- incorporate the guidelines as a model in addition to making the guidelines on official releases and publications by official organizations widely known by encouraging independent efforts on the part of the private media.

All ministries and agencies were to be responsible for the implementation of these measures, the basic aim being to prevent 'a singular emphasis on the sexual aspect of women, the uncritical treatment of violence against women and the perpetuation of gender-based stereotypes in the media' (Headquarters for the Promotion of Gender Equality Japan 1996). A subsequent report on progress indicated that some local public organizations had already formulated their guidelines for achieving these aims.

As far as the media organizations themselves were concerned, the Plan of Action stipulated only that voluntary efforts on the part of the media were to be encouraged. The document, being a government production, was not of course binding on the private sector, any more than the postwar script policies had been. In the latter case, however, the government policies were welcomed and implemented: it was in the best interests of the press to comply with reforms that were being put into effect in the education system of their future readers and that could be expected to improve both the efficiency of production and their circulation figures. In the case of gender, by 1996 the media were able to point to their 'iikaeshū' as evidence that they were already taking account of the actual words used about women, if not the stereotypical portrayal of gender roles in reporting. Media reports about women in Japan, as elsewhere, still often focused on gender-specific details irrelevant to the incident at hand. In the case of suspects in a crime, Shikata (1998) notes, phrases occur like 'mainly cooks frozen foods' or 'rooms full of dust', reflecting on housewifely skills, or 'pregnant but not to her husband' and 'has had an abortion', reflecting on sexual behaviour. Victims fare little better, with comments on their dress, appearance and relationships with men being commonplace.

In an interview conducted for this research in 2001, the former director of the Gender Equality Bureau remarked that use of 'sabetsu yōgo' itself had decreased markedly: for example, newspapers no longer referred to women over 60 as 'rōjo' or commented on the personal appearance of professional women. As a result of growing awareness of the social influence of the actual words used about women, such language is no longer a particular concern, in formal discourse at least. Of more concern is the continuing confusion over gender role allocation in language: for example, when someone says that a certain way of speaking is not 'josei rashii' (womanly) or that women like to speak in a certain way. The biggest offenders in this regard, she thought, were in the informal sphere: low-quality TV dramas and commercials which emphasized women's sexual aspects. In other words, the focus had shifted from the actual language used to speak about women in the press and other arenas of public discourse, but the problem of stereotyping, particularly on TV, remained. The government did not, and in the interests of freedom of expression should not, have any control over this, but to see naked women in commercials or women in TV dramas putting up with being abandoned by men did nothing for ideas of gender equality. The most that the Office of Gender Equality could do was issue guidelines. It was difficult for the government to tell the media not to use certain language when women's groups, unlike the BLL, did not take action themselves to protest it, perhaps through a failure of nerve. In her view, women's groups and women researchers should be concentrating their efforts on this informal sphere, since government could do no more than offer guidelines for the formal, public sphere along the lines of not assigning particular characteristics to people on the basis of gender or assuming, for example, that all doctors are male and all nurses are female.

The BLL and disability support groups had shown nerve and tenacity in mounting language protests, reacting strongly to every occasion on which disputed terms had occurred, with the result that they had had great success in changing the language used to refer to them on human rights grounds, so that 'bikko' and similar terms were no longer used. Women's groups, on the other hand, who represented a section of the population much larger than did these other groups – which was perhaps the cause of the problem – had not been as strong (personal interview 2001). We can see this in the continuing use of words embodying patriarchal views of women and gender roles, such as 'shujin' (husband) and 'mibōjin' (widow).

## The words

As with other groups discussed in this book, the words used by society to designate women have been a focus of contention. There are many choices for the word 'woman': 'onna', 'joshi', 'josei', 'fujin' are the most common. Nakamura (1990: 148–161) argues that 'onna' (woman) encapsulates the representation of female sexuality as sex object. Using a series of examples, she shows that 'onna' are defined in sexual terms alone while 'otoko' (men) are defined both as sexual beings and also whole persons. In terms of connotative level of stylistic formality based on whether or not they are Japanese or Sino-Japanese words, stylistic formality being 'closely related to the strength of negative connotations associated with a term', she classifies 'onna', 'josei', 'joshi' and 'fujin' into three groups: 'onna' is the most informal and therefore the most negatively valued; 'joshi' and 'fujin' are the most formal and therefore less negatively valued; and 'josei' lies somewhere in the middle. Nakamura further classifies negative terms used about women into six categories:

1   unmarried woman (e.g. *orudo misu* [old maid], *urenokori* [unsold], *ikiokure* [late to go]);
2   old woman (e.g. *rōba* [old woman], *rōjo* [old woman]);
3   young girl (e.g. *komusume* [small girl]);

4    ugly woman (e.g. *busu, okame, tinkusha*);
5    unfeminine girl (e.g. *otenba* [tomboy], *su(zu)be* [juvenile delin-
     quent], *hanekkaeri* [spring-back]);
6    unfeminine woman (e.g. *joketsu* [woman-brave], *otokomasari*
     [better than a man], *saijo* [intelligent woman]).

The Japanese version of 'housewife' can be either 'okusan' (when directly addressing the person) or 'shufu' (when speaking about her). Ueno (1987: s. 79) describes the contradiction between these two as originating in differing social classes. 'Contradiction arose between the terms *shufu* and *okusan*, the former referring to the head of a peasant work collective and the latter modelled on the samurai family, with its sexual division of labor between bread-winning husbands and child-tending wives, in which women were more reproducers than producers'. The two words today therefore reflect historical structures no longer necessarily relevant, but it is difficult to know what could replace them in everyday discourse. These and other words which constitute women in terms of out-moded gender roles represent the kind of accepted 'common sense' social wisdom which perpetuates gender discrimination in everyday discourse. Language in this way has the power to normalize, main-tain and reproduce discrimination as it lags behind changes in the external world, no longer representing the world as it really is but rather constituting it in terms of a set of past practices which accord with the views of the authorities (Nakamura 1999: 47).

As in English, one of the enduring irritations for women is the use of the words 'onna', 'fujin', 'josei' and 'joryū', all meaning 'female' or 'woman', as prefixes to the generic names of occupations. The names of some work traditionally done by women incorporate an element indicating this (as in 看護婦 'kangofu', nurse, where the final character means a woman); the prefix is added to those which do not (e.g. 'josei bengoshi', woman lawyer, 'fujin keikan', police-woman, 'onna dorobo', female thief). The usual connotation is sur-prise at finding a woman in a profession dominated by men, carrying overtones of 'onna de arinagara'/'onna de aru no ni'/'onna no kuse ni'/'onnadatera ni' (even though she's a woman) (Reynolds 1999: 229–31). By contrast, when domains like nursing are occupied by men, no such prefix is applied: instead, an overt masculine marker is added to the end of the word, for example, 看護士 'kangoshi' for 'male nurse' rather than 看護婦, 'kangofu' (Abe 1995).

The practice of adding prefixes is always discouraged both in media editorial guidelines and in government guidelines for text referring to women, but nevertheless persists: the mere fact that guidelines exist does not mean that they are always honoured. An article in the *Asahi Shimbun*, for example, took exception to the constant prefixing of the word 'josei' to the word 'governor' when Fusae Ota, the first woman to become governor of Osaka, was appointed in 2000. Although prefixing an occupation with the (female) gender of its holder was directly contrary to the advice given in the *Kisha Handobukku*, the journalist pointed out, even such a rudimentary guideline as this was almost daily ignored in practice in Japan's press, thereby reinforcing discrimination on the basis of gender in the public mind (Katō 2000).

What is it that defines a woman? 'Onna rashii' (like a woman) is a contentious phrase which is used to define what behaviours are and are not acceptable for the Japanese concept of a 'good' woman, just as 'otoko rashii' (like a man) delineates the parameters of what men do or should be doing. Falconer (1984: 91) points out that the significance of '-rashii' (-like) behaviour in Japanese society is much greater than in the West, carrying much stronger connotations of expectation and conforming to rules. Although one can conform to more than one type of '-rashii' behaviour (e.g. like a mother, like a daughter, like a wife), the overarching expectation of 'onna-rashii' is not compatible with elements expected of 'otoko-rashii' behaviour; nor can the same person act in both Japanese-like and foreigner-like ways. In other words, the permissible combination of what she calls different 'rashii' is determined by strong social sanctions on what boundaries can be blended or blurred. The term 'onna-rashii' therefore carries very strong overtones of traditional Japanese gender roles for women. For modern women, whose roles have changed on an individual level while social acceptance of that change lags behind, to be described as not being 'onna-rashii' has been identified as a particular source of irritation and friction in feminist discussions of language. The linguistic dimensions of 'onna-rashii' have been questioned in discussions of Japanese women's speech; given that Japanese women today speak in a broad variety of ways, is 'onna-rashii' really relevant any longer as a description or even a set of expectations (Okamoto 1995: 299)?

A large element of 'onna rashii' relates to marital status, i.e. she should be. Unlike terms used to describe women in family relationships, words describing unmarried women have been inventive: 'haimisu' (high miss), 'ōrudo misu' (old miss), 'kurisumasu keeki' (Christmas cake, i.e. best eaten before the twenty-fifth [birthday]) and 'urenokori' (unsold goods) are the most common terms. Such words in the noughties, however, no longer carry the sting they once did, as more and more financially self-sufficient Japanese women choose to remain single rather than settle for second best in the marriage stakes. When they do marry, it is later on average than it used to be: 'the average age for Japanese women marrying for the first time stands at 27.4 years old. Women in their late 20s used to have the highest fertility rate in the past, but now approximately half of women in this age bracket still remain unmarried' (Gender Equality Bureau 2004).

'Shujin' (husband, literally meaning master) has attracted a very great deal of comment and animus because of its patriarchal overtones. If we check the 1955 first edition of the *Kōjien* for 'shujin', we find three meanings given: i) the master of a household; ii) the person one serves, and iii) what a wife ('tsuma') calls her husband ('otto'). These definitions also appear in a revised version of the second edition published in 1976 and again in the 1998 fifth edition, where they are supplemented by two others, one saying that it is a respectful appellation, the other that it can mean someone who looks after guests. The connotation of 'master' in the husband-wife relation remains unchanged and an enduring source of irritation to Japanese feminists. But finding an acceptable alternative can be difficult, as Abe (1995) reports at length:

> Most Japanese feminists including myself resist this word and replace it with more neutral terms such as tsureai, meaning 'someone you are with' and otto 'husband.' However the acceptance of these words in Japan is limited. Therefore, when I talk with a woman for the first time, especially one who is not a feminist or unaware of feminist concerns, I sometimes find myself in a quandary. I do not hesitate to use the term tsureai to refer to my husband, yet I sometimes think twice before using the same word to refer to her husband. My concern with not making the woman uncomfortable outweighs my desire not to use sexist words. Is this behavior 'compromising,' or 'sensitive'? Whichever the case, it is this dilemma I constantly face when speaking.

And yet 'shujin', she continues, citing Endō's book *Ki ni naru Kotoba* (*Disturbing Language*), having first appeared in Japanese-English dictionaries after 1924 and in monolingual Japanese dictionaries after 1955, only came to mean 'husband' comparatively recently; before the war, 'otto' and 'tsureai' were commonly used.

In 1985, the Kotoba to Onna o kangaeru Kai (Women and Language Research Group) published a book which examined words relating to men and to women in eight Japanese language dictionaries published in the previous five years. They did this, they said, to draw attention to the derogatory attitude towards women displayed by the people who wrote the dictionary definitions; such definitions were particularly important given that people rely so much on dictionaries to give 'the truth' about reality. An example: the 1980 third edition of the Iwanami *Kokugo Jiten* defines the word 'umazume' ('stone woman', a derogatory word referring to a woman unable to bear children) as 'a woman without the ability to conceive; a woman who cannot give birth to children'. The authors point out that there is no corresponding word for a childless man. Despite the fact that the cause for infertility often lies with the man, it is the woman who is referred to as cold and hard as stone (Kotoba to Onna o kangaeru Kai 1985: 15–16). 'Shufu' (housewife) was listed with two main meanings: the wife of the head of the house (shujin no tsuma), and the woman who, being a wife, was in charge of running the household. In other words, to identify yourself as a 'shufu' was to say that you were the wife of X and you cooked, cleaned and washed for him and his family (p. 127). As far as being the wife of the 'shujin' went, the authors took issue with the dictionary definition of 'shujin' as 'the master/head of a household or family': once, perhaps, they thought, but not in today's Japan, where men belonged body and soul to the company and only gave their families what little they had left over from that. Their contribution to the household (apart, presumably, from the income they provided) was minimal, and there was little to be proud of in saying you were the wife of such a 'master' (pp. 130–1).

Proverbs often encapsulate attitudes derogatory to women. To give just a small sample, some denigrate female intelligence, for example, 'onna no chie wa hana no saki' (a woman sees no further than the tip of her nose); or belittle female strength, as in 'onna no chikara to kubi no nai ishibotoke' (a woman's strength is as useful as a stone Buddha without a head, i.e. not at all); or paint women as chatterboxes, as in 'onna sannin yoreba kashimashii' (three women together make a racket) and as fickle, as in 'onnagokoro to aki no sora' (a woman's heart and the autumn sky, i.e. both can change quickly). A 1995 book, Watanabe's *Kotowaza ni arawareta Seisabetsu (Gender Discrimination in Proverbs)*, from which these examples are taken, lists many, many more. In general, Watanabe's study found, twice as many proverbs relating to gender deal with men and women in the context of their family roles, as husbands and wives, parents, sons and daughters, brides and grooms, the mother-in-law-daughter-in-law relationship and son on than with men and women in general, showing the strength of the family system (Watanabe 1995: 201). Other examples from the *Asahi Evening News Proverbs* dictionary are 'onna wa sangai ni ie nashi' (once a woman marries, she gives up everything) and 'otto ni sugao mise na' (keep yourself looking good for your husband). Patriarchal expectations of gender roles are deeply ingrained in pro-verbs, which are commonly taken to encapsulate folk wisdom as to 'the way things are' (and by extension, the way they should be). This is not to imply that there are no proverbs which make fun of or diminish men; of course there are. But more than any other group such as people with disabilities or Burakumin, women are subject to fossilization of both character and behavioural expecta-tions in this medium.

## Protests over language and images

Although the lack of activism by women's groups may have been a cause for regret in 2001, as mentioned by the interviewee above, in the 1980s and early 1990s there were in fact quite a few such incidents, though not in the same numbers as the BLL. Despite the government's early lead in the eradication of gendered language in the 1980s, the private sector was slower to follow, with the result that a series of vocal protests from women's action groups marked the same decade during which government documents were being rewritten. Complaints over sexism targeted both representation and language. Advertising became a particular focus of complaint; often the terms themselves were not at issue so much as the message the wording or the visual content conveyed. Women's groups were successful on many occasions in having what they considered to be sexually discriminatory advertising posters withdrawn as a result of organized protest. A 1983 advertisement for instant noodles with a script of 'watashi tsukuru hito' (I am the one who makes them, said by the woman), 'watashi taberu hito' (I am the one who eats them, said by the man) was withdrawn after complaints from the women's movement. An Eidan subway poster was withdrawn a month earlier than planned in 1988 after women's groups complained that its close-up of a woman's legs emphasized women as sex objects. The 1988 Ministry of Postal Services withdrew from post offices nationwide pamphlets featuring women in aprons after complaints from an Osaka women's group that it was no longer appropriate to equate woman with housewife (Takagi 1999: 136, 138, 148).

In 1993, a magazine cover story describing how to coerce female office colleagues into sex against their will became the subject of protests from a group calling itself the Women's Network Against Sexual Violence (STON'90). In a manner reminiscent of responses to BLL denunciations, the publishers admitted fault, met with the group to discuss the matter, and later ran a seminar on sexual discrimination with group members as lecturers. Protests from different groups over other instances, for example, of TV commercials and advertising posters appearing to hint at rape, have led a major advertising agency to set up a monitoring system whereby consumers provide feedback before advertisements are released. Tactics have also included the use of stickers: the Women's Action Group put stickers bearing the character for 'anger' on posters they disapproved of, while the Japan Women's Studies Society affixed stickers saying 'This is discrimination' (Yunomae 1995: 57–8).

Some incidents involved employers. In 1983, for instance, the Kinokuniya company in Tokyo was prosecuted by its labour union for discrimination against women because a confidential company document was discovered to specify among other things that no 'busu' (ugly), 'chibi' (tiny) or 'kappe' (bumpkin) women were to be employed. Other female workers in Tokyo also brought a suit for damages in 1984 claiming that the words 'chibi' and 'busu' were demeaning to women (Takagi 1999: 143). *Time* magazine picked up on the Kinokuniya incident, with the following report:

> A great scandal (prompting the typical Japanese reaction: a resigned and knowing shrug) broke out recently when Fujin Minshu Shimbun, a Tokyo feminist newspaper, published a personnel memo from the office of Kinokuniya Bookstore, one of the nation's largest retailers. The memo listed some warning signs when considering hiring women: ugly women, short women, argumentative women, divorcees, women interested in reformist politics, women who 'respect passionate artists like Van Gogh' – in fact, practically [all] women. Nevertheless, nearly half of Kinokuniya's employees are women, 60 per cent of whom work part-time.
>
> (O'Reilly 1983: 69)

Eliminating prejudices based on ideas of relative worth of the sexes was not simply a matter of stereotyping in the media, of course, but went much deeper to an examination of the language itself, in which women's inferiority is deeply enshrined at both the lexical and semantic levels. Women and children are often treated as a single unit ('onnakodomo', women and children) and weak actions are described in terms of women, for example, 'onna no yō ni' (like a woman), 'onna rashii' (like a woman) and other similar expressions, as we have seen. Women's groups have long protested the use of the word 'shujin' (master) for husband and 'okusan/kanai' (inside the house) for wife, not to mention 'mibōjin' (not yet dead person) for widow.

## The media arrive (late)

By 1994, some progress had been made in the visibility of women in the 'iikaeshū', in which they had previously hardly figured at all. The *Asahi Shimbun*'s list (reproduced in Takagi 1999: 296–302) had expanded to include six entries in a separate section entitled 'Seisabetsugo' (gender-discriminatory words): the contested 'mibōjin' was to be replaced by 'koXXXshi no tsuma' (wife of the late Mr XXX); 'joryū' (female) was not to be used to prefix an occupation 'except where absolutely necessary'; 'joketsu' and 'jojōfu' (both meaning 'heroine' or 'outstanding woman') were not to be used at all; nor were 'onnagotoki ga', 'onna no kuse ni', 'onnadatera' and 'onna-nagaramo' (even though she's a woman); 'japayuki-san' (a word used to indicate Asian prostitutes coming to Japan) was to be changed to 'Ajiajin nyūkokusha' (Asian immigrants); and finally, 'shujin' and 'teishu' (another word meaning 'master' and by extension 'husband') were to be changed to 'otto' wherever possible. This was a case of too little too late, however, for Saitō Masami, a member of the Media no naka no Seisabetsu o kangaeru Kai (Gender Discrimination in the Media Study Group). Having discovered that the *Kisha Handobukku* and the stylebooks for three of the major dailies contained no satisfactory discussion of discrimination and its manifestations, she turned to the in-house collections, including those of the *Asahi* (1994, discussed above), the *Mainichi* (1992) and the *Yomiuri* (1993). None of them except the *Mainichi* list attempted to define discrimination; instead, they listed words to be mechanically replaced wherever they occurred, i.e. independent of context. All three companies listed less than 20 words relating to gender discrimination (Saitō 1997).

The following year, high-profile Japanese feminist Ueno Chizuko and the Media no naka no Seisabetsu o kangaeru Kai published a book called *Kitto Kaerareru Seisabetsugo: Watashi-tachi no Gaidorain* (*Gender-discriminatory Language that can Certainly be Changed: Our Guidelines*). The foundation principles of the book, as outlined in the preface, are that language is power; that it is a changing, living thing; that media language is extremely influential in the public sphere; that there is a power differential between media writers and readers, and that readers need to let media know if the message being sent is not an appropriate one and request a change; and that far from being an attack on freedom of expression, or suggesting that speech should be regulated by law, this book's guidelines are no more than proposals from citizens about language use. Guidelines are not regulations; they are a set of suggestions to journalists to think about how they should responsibly wield the power the media gives them to influence society.

The book is divided into chapters, liberally furnished with examples from the press, dealing with:

* 43 disputed appellations for women, including OL (office lady), 'shufu' (housewife), 'kyariaredii' (career woman), 'otome' (virgin, maiden), 'mibōjin' (widow), 'bijin' (beautiful woman) and the usual range of words indicating that the person performing a certain occupation is female, for example, 'shufu sakka' (housewife author), 'josei taishi' (woman ambassador), 'joyū' (actress).

* Lists of expressions encapsulating a particular image of women, like 'shojosaku' (maiden work, for one's first published book), 'nyōbōyaku' (one's righthand man, where 'nyōbō' is a word for wife, implying that someone's main 'helper' plays a role equivalent to that of a wife, i.e. subsidiary), 'josei sukandaru' (woman scandal, when reporting the amorous affairs of politicians and other prominent men, as if the affairs were the women's fault), and 'bokoku' (mother country, as if only women were responsible for procreation).

* Representations of women in language which assume they will be in a subordinate position, such as 'uchi josei 3nin' (including 3 women, seen in a report on the number of people who had passed the foreign service examination), 'mikon no haha' (unmarried mother, used when reporting women's exploits, an unnecessary invasion of privacy), 'yamato nadeshiko' (an old term for the ideal form of Japanese womanhood).

* Words expressing or implying traditional gender role expectations, such as that even in the workplace women will be in

supporting roles to men, for example, 'otokomasari' (a woman of masculine spirit, when a woman does very well, connotation of surprise that she should outperform men), 'ofukuro no aji' (just like mum's home cooking), 'hataraku josei' (working woman, ignores the fact that women at home work hard as well).

- Special treatment of men in language, such as the much-disputed 'shujin' (husband), the use of the prefix 'male' with words like 'childrearing' and other traditionally female domains (which implies that men doing this are somehow worthy of special notice, whereas women are not), and the creation of words like 'kangoshi' (nurse, male) replacing 'kangofu' (nurse, female) when no similar words were created when women first entered traditionally male spheres of work.

In some cases, neutral alternatives to disputed words are suggested, for example, 'wakai josei' (young woman) for 'otome', 'otto o nakushita hito' (someone who has lost her husband) for 'mibōjin', 'hatsu sakuhin' (first published work) for 'shojosaku', 'shusshinkoku' (country of origin) for 'bokoku' and 'dokushin' single) for 'unmarried'. In others, it is suggested that the expressions be dropped altogether. With regard to occupations, only generic terms which give no indication of gender should be used in the media. The book concludes with chapters on language change and social change (using the United States as the example) and a comparison of the American movement against gender-discriminatory language and the Japanese situation.

Perhaps resulting from the publication of this book, the 1997 edition of the *Kisha Handobukku* for the first time included guidelines on avoiding gender discrimination in writing, with a category 'seisabetsugo' (gender-discriminatory words) added to the lists of words to be avoided relating to race, status, occupation and disability (Saitō 1997). The category was fairly rudimentary: journalists were advised to avoid the prefix 'joryū' before occupations, use the neutral 'san' rather than the gender-specific 'joshi' following women's names, change 'fukei' and 'fujin keikan' (both 'policewoman') to 'josei keikan' (still 'policewoman', but substituting the preferred term for 'woman'), and avoid expressions which placed undue emphasis on (particularly female) gender such as 'joketsu' (heroine) and 'onnadatera ni' (even though she's a woman) (Kyōdō Tsūshinsha 1999: 84–5). The other journalists' bible, Jiji Tsūshin's *Saishin Yōji Yōgo Bukku* (*Handbook of Up-to-date Characters and Words*), did not follow the *Kisha Handobukku* down this track. Its advice on 'sabetsugo' contained no separate category pertaining to gender, and only the standard words which had featured in the early 1970s lists (e.g. 'jochū','mekake', 'rōba', 'jokō') featured in its list, betraying a lack of awareness of – or at least, a lack of awareness of the relationship to language of – the gender-related social changes which had occurred during the intervening years (Jiji Tsūshinsha 1997: 525–7).

*Kitto Kaerareru Seisabetsugo* came in for some criticism in *Hōsō Repōto* (*Broadcasting Report*), in part on the grounds that such changes would impoverish the language. The unnamed writer who said this argued that Japanese had been 'yutaka' (rich) until now, but that thanks to language reform movements 'minorities' were now increasingly attacking traditional expressions. Unwieldy euphemisms aimed at avoiding offence to minorities were a blight upon the quality of the language. Members of the Media no Naka no Seisabetsu o kangaeru Kai took issue with this claim, retorting that their critic's definition of 'yutaka' was too circumscribed; a real 'yutaka na hyōgen' in fact builds a just and fair society rather than excluding sections of it.

Changes in the language used about women have been slow in coming, reflecting the extent to which – perhaps more than the other groups – the language relating to them encapsulates centuries of deeply-ingrained accepted social wisdom as to their roles and characteristics. To change this is therefore a much greater challenge to 'jōshiki' than is the case with ethnicity, status or disability-related terms, given the much greater percentage of the population occupied by women.

# CONCLUSION

The discussion on language is bound to continue in Japan, as else-where: the internet, if nothing else, will see to that. The tactics which worked well for the BLL and other activist groups in target-ing media, publishers and bookstores to force compliance through embarrassment will continue; we saw in Chapter 3 that Zenkokuren, the new Burakumin activist group formed in 1992, has carried out a denunciation of Channel 2. Given the dispersed nature of ISPs, which could be anywhere in the world, however, it is not so easy to apply the formerly proven tactics. Action on a more international scale is needed, and the BLL, through its international arm IMADR, has not been slow to call on the United Nations to address the issue. This approach has had some success already, when a provider shut down an anti-Burakumin site after being presented with two English-language documents, one a resolution of the United Nations and the other a paper on discrimination against Burakumin in Japan. The summary report on that case reflected:

> This case shows us that ISPs may not respond to a request made by just one grassroots group but may do so when they realize that this problem is so serious that even the United Nations takes it into serious consideration. As a result, the Network learned a new way to approach ISPs and got another discriminatory website named the 'Shin Jiyū Kyōkai' (or the Association of True Liberties), which we had observed for two years, finally deleted when we sent the same documents to the ISP.
>
> (Tabata 2000)

Hate speech may have moved online, but it has not done so unpursued. The racist and other rantings which pepper Channel 2

135

postings are frequently challenged in robust terms by other contributors, as well as through more formal channels as a result of the
watching brief kept by the NDRH as described in Chapter 2.

As we have seen in the foregoing chapters, language and linguistic stereotyping relating to minorities have been successfully
contested through a variety of means. Today's media and publishing
houses sanitize their language by using neutral terms when referring
to aspects of difference, or – in the case of Burakumin – try to avoid
referring to them at all. Of all the groups discussed here, women have
had the smallest degree of success: guidelines on gender-neutral
language were late in coming and are often honoured in the breach,
whereas language use about other groups is more prudently observed,
partly because women have been less vocal on this point than others
and partly because the language relating to women carries very
deeply entrenched patriarchal attitudes about 'the way things should
be' in relation to gender roles. Whereas language relating to disability
or ethnicity encapsulates stigma based on physical or mental difference in the case of the former and historical legacies in the case
of the latter, linguistic appellations for or descriptions of women
are part of majority society's 'common sense' view of the natural
order of things, despite the changes in that order wrought over the
past century, and in particular the last 50 years.

International movements on several fronts assisted either tangen-
tially or directly in the development of more inclusive language,
or at least, language more acceptable to those to whom it referred.
The United Nations International Year of Disabled Persons was a
key factor in the revision of terminology in statutes; the women's
movement and the United Nations Decade for Women helped raise
awareness of at least the issues relating to language and women, if
not immediate change, though in the area of visual representation
of women protests brought some changes. For the Ainu people, it
was the growing activism of indigenous groups around the world in
the 1980s and the accompanying legal principles that began to emerge
as rights that was a key factor leading to the Sapporo Court decision which saw them recognized as an ethnic minority.

Although the last of these factors also helped Burakumin groups
further bring their status to international attention, it was this group
which did the groundwork for the others much earlier in the twentieth century after the Suiheisha took the decision to confront and
protest derogatory references to themselves in print or in the nascent
NHK broadcasting system. Through the strategy of denunciation,
at times belligerent, they became feared by publishers to the extent

that the very first 'iikaeshū', as we have seen, included Burakumin-related terms and (related) terms for occupation as their first, and sometimes only, component. Whether the denunciation strategy achieved its aims is hard to say, given that it certainly saw the demise of derogatory language or stereotyping in the print and visual media but at the cost of almost total silence about Burakumin issues, reinforcing the 'put a lid on a stink' or 'don't wake a sleeping child' folk wisdom surrounding this issue.

It is difficult to imagine how the other groups would have achieved media compliance with their requests had it not been for the example set by the BLL's relentless campaign. If the price of liberty is eternal vigilance, then the same, it would seem, is true of the price of respect. Given the culture of shame in Japan, with public embarrassment a prospect greatly to be avoided, the constant and very vocal protests over language were sufficient to persuade the media to comply by drawing up their lists of words to be avoided or replaced. The mechanical nature of these substitutions, avoiding certain words on the basis of protests without any real consideration or discussion of why they were discriminatory, has drawn criticism from some who would have preferred a more open and extended debate on discrimination. It is evident, however, from the amount of discussion of 'sabetsugo' on internet chat groups and the large number of books published on the issue, that the word lists have caused people to think about language use, even if they do not agree with the self-regulatory measures taken. To that extent, then, they have played a useful part.

Editorial self-regulation continues in 2004. Responses from major publishers surveyed for this research indicated that, while most did not have formal lists like the newspapers and broadcasters, editors-in-chief are responsible for checking for 'sabetsu hyōgen' and exercising their own good judgement on the issue. Where a question arises, they consult with the company's legal department, which then makes the decision on a case by case basis, having regard to the writer's freedom of expression. Some companies participate in the activities of the 'Shuppan Jinken Sabetsu Mondai Kondankai' (Publishers Human Rights Discrimination Issues Group), a group of 38 publishing companies which regularly holds lectures and meetings and study groups to ensure that discriminatory language use does not occur. Others reported that they had learned from previous experiences with protests and now carried out stringent checks. One very large publishing house was quite specific: in arriving at a judgement on whether a passage is discriminatory or not, its editors check not just the words themselves but the ideas being expressed. If something is judged to be discriminatory, the publisher talks with the writer and after that decides whether to delete the words or substitute something different, or even sometimes halt publication.

We saw in Chapter 1 that no definitions of 'sabetsugo', 'sabetsu yōgo' and 'sabetsu hyōgen' appeared in the first (1955) and second (1969) editions of the *Kōjien*. That is not surprising, as the debate about discriminatory language had not yet really begun to heat up. What is really surprising, however, is that these terms are not defined in the 1998 fifth edition, given the amount of debate over the issue in the 1980s and 1990s.

External measures of discrimination appear to be gradually weakening with the development of government policies and laws such as the Special Measures Law for improvement of Burakumin living conditions, the Equal Employment Opportunity Law and the Basic Law for a Gender-Equal Society, the Fundamental Law for Disabled Persons, the Ainu Cultural Promotion Act and the removal of the fingerprinting requirement for resident foreigners. Social discrimination, however, is harder to eradicate. The fight over language and stereotyping has been an attempt to come to grips with one of its most obvious manifestations, and the one most intimately related to everyday life.

Online hate speech and the introduction of a racial vilification law are the two areas likely to develop as the foci of debate in this area over the coming ten years. Both relate closely to the constitutionally enshrined freedom of speech, as we saw in earlier chapters. It all boils down to human rights versus freedom of speech, and to what extent it may be possible to reach an accommodation with each which will be satisfactory to the majority. Whether Japan will bow to international pressure and enact such legislation as UNCERD stipulates, and whether it will prove possible to exert some measure of control over vilification on the internet, will play out in the coming decade as the next stage of the debate over language and discrimination.

# NOTES

## 1 LANGUAGE AND REPRESENTATION: THE GUIDELINES

1 See, e.g. Queensland Public Sector Management Commission (1991) and Pauwels (1991).

## 2 THE FLOW-ON EFFECTS

1 These examples are taken from a Channel 2 thread talking about people with Down's syndrome, http://yasai.2ch.net/company/kako/982/982938712.html, 22 November 2004.
2 See, for example, http://yasai.2ch.net/company/kako/982/982889520.html and http://yasai.2ch.net/company/kako/982/982938712.html, both 22 November 2004.
3 The NDRH deals only with Burakumin-related discrimination, as it explains on a linking page (http://tokyo.cool.ne.jp/human_lights/, 11 December 2002) to another Burakumin-related organization named Human Lights (http://tokyo.cool.ne.jp/human_lights/index-japanese.html, 11 December 2002).
4 Found at http://homepage2.nifty.com/INDI/ (11 December 2002).
5 Although the INDI document refers to it as the New Media Human Rights Institution, this organization's own website gives its English name as the New Media Human Rights Organization (http://www.jinken.ne.jp/about/kiyaku.html, 11 December 2002).
6 http://www.jinken.ne.jp/ (11 December 2002).
7 See http://hyper1.amuser-net.ne.jp/~auto1/bbsgrp1/bbs10/usr/VEV01463/brd1/dengon.cgi?callnum=refread&orgnum=927&email=&wtpass (12 December 2002).

## 3 STATUS DISCRIMINATION

1 The word 'dōwa' means 'assimilation' and is used as an administrative term to refer to Burakumin issues.
2 Employers were found to be buying these lists, which included details of Buraku place names, locations and main occupations from all over Japan, from direct mail suppliers at a cost of between ¥5,000 and ¥50,000.

Purchasers were in the main large corporations – including Toyota, Nissan and others, wishing to weed out possible Burakumin applicants for positions. The BLL began denunciations of this practice from 1977 on.

3 Ooms (1996: 243–4) reports that this term was not used to describe themselves by those to whom it referred; instead, they used the word 'kawata' (leather workers), denoting their main occupation.

4 Brameld (1968: 124) notes that 'four has long been the supremely insulting number to *burakumin*', citing fights over people being referred to as 'the square root of 16' or even B29 (a four-engined plane).

5 http://www.liberty.or.jp/index2.html, 12 December 2002.

6 Much the same sort of practice of covert identification can be seen today in the manner in which the births of illegitimate children are registered: instead of being listed as 'first son', 'second son', 'first daughter' or whatever position the child is born into in the family, children born out of wedlock are registered simply as 'child', a sure sign of illegitimacy (Stevens 2001: 187). This practice was highlighted as discriminatory by the United Nations Human Rights Commission in its response to Japan's fourth periodic report under Article 40 of the covenant in 1998 (MOFA 1998, item 12).

7 Fukuoka (Isomura and Fukuoka 1994: 29–30) notes that since the 1970s, the media have treated the term 'buraku' in three ways: using it to refer to a village community whether or not it is a Burakumin community; when referring to Burakumin villages, using the words 'tokushu chiku' (special area) or 'tokushu chitai' (special region) instead; or avoiding the word altogether whether referring to Burakumin villages or not.

8 http://homepage3.nifty.com/na-page/, 4 December 2004.

9 International Movement Against Discrimination and Racism, an NGO founded by the BLL in 1988 which has consultative status with the United Nations Economic and Social Council.

10 The NDRH deals only with Burakumin-related discrimination, as it explains on a linking page (http://tokyo.cool.ne.jp/human_lights/, 11 December 2002) to another Burakumin-related organization named Human Lights (http://tokyo.cool.ne.jp/human_lights/index-japanese.html, 11 December 2002).

11 http://www.nichibenren.or.jp/en/activities/meetings/200203151.html.

12 http://village.infoweb.ne.jp/~jclu/katsudou/seimei_ikensho/20021108.html.

13 http://www.japanpen.or.jp/honkan/seimei/020509.html.


## 4 ETHNICITY

1 Use of this term in a Hokkaido shop's name coupled with an Ainu image led to a protest against the business which saw the shop renamed. The argument of the protesters was that the word was no longer valid to describe Ainu people (Sala 1975: 63).

2 Although they could and did apply to private and prefectural/municipal universities (Fukuoka 2000: 26).

3 The thread may be found at http://search.luky.org/fol.1999/msg00627.html (accessed 9 December 2004).

4 See, e.g. http://www.geocities.co.jp/CollegeLife-Labo/8108/ishihara-e.htm (accessed 1 March 2004).
5 See http://blhrri.org/blhrri_e/news/new113/new11301.html (accessed 1 March 2004).
6 This information and that in the following paragraph comes from articles published in *The Japan Times* in April 2000.
7 http://www.issho.org/.
8 http://www.debito.org/.

## 5 DISABILITY

1 http://human5.2ch.net/test/read.cgi/handicap/1102240761/l50, 15 December 2004.

## 6 GENDER

1 Online at http://www.gender.go.jp/koudou/english/, accessed 10 December 2000.

# REFERENCES

Abe, H. (1995) 'From stereotype to context: the study of Japanese women's speech', *Feminist Studies*, 21(3): 647–72.

Ainu Association of Hokkaido (1988) 'Japan's suppression of Ainu Moshiri', *Fourth World Journal*, 4(1): August. Online at www.cwis.org/fwj/22/ainusupp.htm (accessed 18 December 2004).

—— (1989) *A Statement of Opinion Regarding the Partial Revision of I.L.O. Convention No. 107.* Online at ftp://ftp.halcyon.com/pub/FWDP/Eurasia/ainu.txt (accessed 18 December 2004).

Aldwinckle, D. (1996) *A Snipe at Bilingual Non-Japanese on Japanese National TV.* Online at www.debito.org/kumegaffeone.html (accessed 9 December 2004).

Alford, P. (2004) 'The name on almost every Japanese woman's lips', *The Australian*, 22 November: 12.

Andersson, R. (2000) *Burakumin and Shimazaki Tōson's Hakai: Images of Discrimination in Modern Japanese Literature.* Lund: Department of East Asian Languages, Lund University. Online at www.lub.lu.se/luft/diss/hum119.pdf (accessed 20 November 2004).

*Asahi Shimbun* (1997) http://www.ex.media.osaka-cu.ac.jp/~97j100 donguri.html (accessed 2 May 2000).

—— (2003) 'Sapporo-shi, "shōgaisha" aratame "shōgaisha"' (In Sapporo, 'shōgaisha' changes to 'shōgaisha'), 18 July. Online at http://mytown.asahi.com/hokkaido/news02.asp?kiji=5235 (accessed 16 December 2004).

Baba, Y. (1980) 'A study of minority-majority relations; the Ainu and Japanese in Hokkaido', *The Japan Interpreter* 13(1): 60–92.

Bailey, J. (1998) 'Behind the scenes: political correctness stifles showbiz subtitlers', *Tokyo Weekender*. Online at www/weekender.co.jp/LatestEdition/981204/behind.html (accessed 16 December 2004).

Batchelor, J. (1892) *The Ainu of Japan: The Religions, Superstitions and General History of the Hairy Aborigines of Japan.* London: Religious Tract Society.

Benson, P. (2001) *Ethnocentrism and the English Dictionary.* London: Routledge.

Bodiford, W. (1996) 'Zen and the art of religious prejudice: efforts to reform a tradition of social discrimination', *Japanese Journal of Religious Studies*, 23(1–2): 1–27.

Bogdanowicz, T. (2003) 'Where are the Ainu now? In search of answers about Japan's indigenous people', *Japan Times Online*, 2 March. Online at www.japantimes.co.jp/cgi-bin/getarticle.pl5?fl20030302a3.htm (accessed 7 December 2004).

Boletta, W. (1992) 'Prescriptivism, politics and lexicography: a reply to Jane Barnes Mack', *ILT News*, 92: 103–11. Online at www.isc.senshu-u.ac.jp/~thb0422/bolehome/downloads/prepollx.pdf (accessed 26 August 2004).

Brameld, T. (1968) *Culture, Education, and Change in Two Communities*. New York: Holt, Rinehart & Winston.

Bryant, T. (1991) 'For the sake of the country, for the sake of the family: the oppressive impact of family registration on women and minorities in Japan', *UCLA Law Review*, 39(1): 109–68.

Buraku Kaihō Dōmei Chūō Honbu (eds) (1988) *Sabetsu Hyōgen to Kyūdan* (*Discriminatory Expressions and Denunciation*). Osaka: Kaihō Shuppansha.

Buraku Kaihō Dōmei Chūō Honbu Shokikyoku (eds) (1976) *Sabetsugo Mondai ni tsuite no Wareware no Kenkai* (*Our Views on the Problem of Discriminatory Language*). Osaka: Kaihō Shimbun Shuppansha.

Buraku Kaihō Kenkūjo (eds) (1980) *Buraku Kaihō Undō Kiso Shiryōshū v.1: Zenkoku Taikai Undō Hōshin Dai 1–20 Kai* (*Buraku Liberation Movement Basic Data v.1: Policies of the National Meeting Movement nos 1–20*). Osaka: Kaihō Shuppansha.

Buraku Liberation and Human Rights Research Institute (1997) 'A man who made discriminatory scribbles found guilty', *Buraku Liberation News*, 99. Online at http://blhrri.org/ blhrri_e/news/new099/new09903.htm (accessed 3 December 2004).

—— (1998) 'Discriminatory graffiti were found twice on the entrance of the Buraku Liberation Center', *Buraku Liberation News*, 102. Online at http://blhrri.org/blhrri_e/news/new102/new10204.htm (accessed 3 December 2004).

—— (2000) 'A student did not regret his series of discriminatory behaviors even after persuaded by the university authorities', *Buraku Liberation News*, 113. Online at www.blhrri.org/blhrri_e/news/new113/new113.html (accessed 18 December 2004).

—— (2002a) 'Sabetsu rakugaki ga hakkaku shi kakunin gakushūkai' ('Confirmation and and study meeting held after discriminatory graffiti comes to light'), *Kaihō Shimbun*, 21 October. Online at www.bll.gr.jp/news2002/news20021021-3.html (accessed 3 December 2004).

—— (2002b) 'Mata mo sabetsu tōsho' ('Another discriminatory letter'), *Kaihō Shimbun*, 4 November. Online at www.bll.gr.jp/news2002/news20021104-4.html (accessed 3 December 2004).

Buraku Liberation League (1998) *Anata mo Shiraberarete iru: Sabetsu ChōsaJiken no Shinsō* (*You too are Being Checked Out: The Truth About Incidents of Discriminatory Checking*). Osaka: Buraku Kaihō Dōmei Chūō Honbu.

—— (2001) *Draft Proposals for the Eradication of Propaganda/Agitation for Buraku Discrimination on the Internet*. Online at www.blhrri.orgblhrri_e/other/006_e.htm (accessed 16 November 2004).

—— (2002a) *'Buraku Chimei Sōkan' Jiken* (*The 'Buraku Chimei Sōkan' Affair*). Online at www.bll.gr.jp/siryositu/s-sbet-sokan.html (accessed 17 December 2004).

—— (2002b) 'NGO report in response to the first and second report prepared by the government of Japan concerning CERD', part 4, *Buraku Liberation News*, 121. Online at www.blhrri.org/blhrri_e/news/new121/new12103.html (accessed 17 December 2004).

—— (2002c) *Sabetsu Kyūdan Tōsō to wa* (*What are Denunciation of Discrimination Conflicts?*). Online at www.bll.gr.jp/kaisetu-kydan.html (accessed 4 December 2002). The English version may be found at http://blhrri.org/blhrri_e/blhrri/q&a.htm#What%20is%20Denunciation? (accessed 4 December 2004).

—— (2002d) *What is Buraku Discrimination?* Online at www.bll.gr.jp/eng.html (accessed 29 November 2004).

—— (2002e) 'NGO report in response to the first and second report prepared by the government of Japan concerning CERD', part 5, *Buraku Liberation News*, 122. Online at www.blhrri.org/blhrri_e/news/new122/new12205.html (accessed 6 December 2004).

Burchfield, R. (1989) *Unlocking the English Language*. London: Faber & Faber.

Cameron, D. (1995) *Verbal Hygiene*. London: Routledge.

Cameron, D. (1998) 'Lost in translation: non-sexist language', in D. Cameron (ed.) *The Feminist Critique of Language: A Reader*. London: Routledge, pp. 155–63.

CERD (2000a) *Reports Submitted by States Parties Under Article 9 of the Convention: Second Periodic Reports of States Parties due in 1999, Addendum, Japan*, CERD/C/350/Add.2. Online at www.unhchr.ch/tbs/doc.nsf/ (accessed 25 November 2004).

—— (2000b) *Concluding Observations of the Committee on the Elimination of Racial Discrimination*, CERD/C/304/Add.114. Online at www.unhchr.ch/tbs/doc.nsf/ (accessed 25 November 2004).

—— (2001) *Summary record of the 1443rd meeting: Japan. 15/03/2000, CERD/C/SR.1443*. Online at http://193.194.138.190/tbs/doc.nsf/0/7000293a6b1f4e09c1256a17005a3efc?Opendocument (accessed 5 December 2004).

Chang, Y. (1998) *Japan Chinatown Changes, But Culture Lives On*. Online at http://huaren.org/ (accessed 23 February 2004).

Channel 2 discussion thread (2001) *Mō 'Shōgaisha* (障害者)*' wa tsukaimasen* (*We Won't Use 'Shōgaisha' Any More*). Online at http://saki.2ch.net/news/kako/986/986344919.html (accessed 16 December 2004).

Chikap, M. (1991) *Kaze no Megumi: Ainu Minzoku no Bunka to Jinken* (*The Blessing of the Wind: The Ainu People's Culture and Rights*). Tokyo: Ochanomizu Shobo.

Chiri, M. (1993) 'False images: the Ainu in school textbooks', *AMPO*, 24(3): 19–22.

Coopman, S. (2000) 'Disability on the Net', *American Communication Journal*, 3(3). Online at www.roguecom.com/roguescholar/scoopman.html (accessed 16 December 2004).

Corker, M. and French, S. (eds) (1999) *Disability Discourse*. Buckingham: Open University Press.

*Courier Mail* (2001a) 'Racist rabbit', 6 May.

—— (2001b) 'Still sour over the kraut word', 25 October.

Dainikai Bunka Fuoramu (1997) Online at www.gakushuin.ac.jp/~19760200/doc.nsf/ (accessed 25 November 2004).

Doyle, M. (1998) 'Introduction to *The A–Z of Non-Sexist Language*', in D. Cameron (ed.) *The Feminist Critique of Language: A Reader*. London: Routledge, pp. 149–54.

DPI-JAPAN (1999) *Country Reports of DPI-Japan 1990–1999*. Online at http://homepage2.nifty.com/ADI/ (accessed 16 December 2004).

Ehrlich, S. and King, R. (1998) 'Gender-based language reform and the social construction of meaning', in D. Cameron (ed.) *The Feminist Critique of Language: A Reader*. London: Routledge, pp. 164–79.

Endō, O. (1993) 'Sexism in Japanese Language Dictionaries', *Japan Quarterly*, 40(4): 395–8.

Falconer, E. (1984) 'Considering Onna-rashii: its importance, enforcement, and effects', *Bulletin of the Graduate School of International Relations*, International University of Japan, 2: 91–103.

Fasold, R. (1987) 'Language policy and change: sexist language in the periodical news media', *Georgetown University Round Table on Languages and Linguistics 1987*. Georgetown University: Washington DC, pp. 187–206.

Fasold, R., Yamada, H., Robinson, D. and Barish, S. (1990) 'The language-planning effect of newspaper editorial policy: gender differences in *The Washington Post*', *Language in Society*, 19: 521–39.

Fogel, J. (1995) *The Cultural Dimension of Sino-Japanese Relations*. Armonk, NY: M.E. Sharpe.

Fowler, E. (2000) 'The *Buraku* in modern Japanese literature: texts and contexts', *Journal of Japanese Studies*, 26(1): 1–39.

French, H. (1999) 'Disdainful of foreigners, the Japanese blame them for crime', *New York Times*, 30 September.

Fukuoka, Y. (1996) *Koreans in Japan: Past and Present*. Online at www.han.org/a/fukuoka96a.html (accessed 9 December 2004).

—— (2000) *Lives of Young Koreans in Japan*, tr. T. Gill. Melbourne: Trans Pacific Press.

Fukuoka, Y. and Tsujiyama, Y. (1992) *Mintohren: Young Koreans against Ethnic Discrimination in Japan*. Online at www.han.org/a/fukuoka92.html (accessed 20 November 2004).

FWCW (n.d.) *FWCW Platform for Action: Women and the Media*. Online at http://www.un.org/womenwatch/daw/beijing/platform/media.htm (accessed 10 December 2004).

Gally, T. (2003) *Lexical Leavings*. Online at www.gally.net/leavings/00/0078.html (accessed 17 December 2004).

Gekkan 'Tsukuru' Henshūbu (1995) *Tsutsui Yasutaka 'Dampitsu' meguru Daironsō* (*The Debate About Tsutsui Yasutaka's Decision to Stop Writing*). Tokyo: Tsukuru Shuppan.

Gender Equality Bureau (2004) *Women in Japan Today 2004: Statistics and Figures*. Online at www.gender.go.jp/english_contents/women2004/statistics/s02.html (accessed 13 December 2004).

Gottlieb, N. (1995) *Word-processing Technology in Japan: Kanji and the Keyboard*. Surrey: Curzon Press.

Gottlieb, N. (1998) 'Discriminatory language in Japan: Burakumin, the disabled and women', *Asian Studies Review*, 22(2): 157–74.

Hanazaki, K. (1996) 'Ainu Moshir and Yaponesia: Ainu and Okinawan identities in contemporary Japan', in D. Denoon, M. Hudson, G. McCormack and T. Morris-Suzuki (eds) *Multicultural Japan: Palaeolithic to Postmodern*. Cambridge: Cambridge University Press, pp. 117–31.

Hane, M. (1982) *Peasants, Rebels and Outcastes: The Underside of Modern Japan*. New York: Pantheon.

Headquarters for the Promotion of Gender Equality Japan (1996) *Plan for Gender Equality 2000: Respect for Human Rights of Women in the Media*. Online at http://www.gender.go.jp/koudou/english/part2-8.html (accessed 10 December 2004).

Heyer, K. (2000) 'From special needs to equal rights: Japanese disability law', *Asian-Pacific Law and Policy Journal*, 1. Online at www.hawaii.edu/aplpj/pdfs/07-heyer.pdf (accessed 16 December 2004).

Hill, R. (1995) 'Approved English only', *The Bulletin*, 14 March: 34.

Hirasawa, Y. (1991) 'The education of minority group children in Japan', in B. Finkelstein, A. Imamura and J. Tobin (eds) *Transcending Stereotypes: Discovering Japanese Culture and Education*. Yarmouth, ME: Intercultural Press, pp. 197–204.

Hoffman, D. (1992) 'Changing faces, changing places: the new Koreans in Japan', *Japan Quarterly*, 39(4): 479–89.

Hokkaidō Utari Kyōkai (n.d.) *Watashi-tachi ni tsuite: Ainu no Seikatsu Jittai* (*About Us: Ainu Life Today*). Online at www.ainu-assn.or.jp/about03.html (accessed 7 December 2004).

Howell, D. (1994) 'Ainu ethnicity and the boundaries of the early modern Japanese state', *Past and Present*, 142: 69–93.

Isomura, E. and Fukuoka, Y. (1994) *Masukomi to Sabetsugo Mondai* (*The Mass Media and Discriminatory Language*). Tokyo: Akashi Shoten.

ISSHO (1996) *Preferring 'Gaijin' Who Speak Poor Japanese*. Online at www.debito.org/kumeISSHOlettereng.html (accessed 9 December 2004).

Jiji Tsūshinsha (ed.) (1997) *Saishin Yōji Yōgo Bukku* (Handbook of Up-to-date Characters and Words). Tokyo: Jiji Tsūshinsha.

*Kaihō Shimbun* (2002) 'Josei ga Jidai o Tsukurō' ('Women will create the era'), 14 October. Online at www.bll.gr.jp/news2002/news20021014-2.html (accessed 2 December 2002).

Kamimura, S., Ikoma, C. and Nakano, S. (2003) *The Japanese and Television, 2000: The Current State of TV Viewing*, Public Opinion Research Division, Japan Broadcasting Corporation. Online at www.nhk.or.jp/bunken/bcri-fr/h13-f1.html (accessed 19 August 2004).

Kaneko, M. (1981) 'Some reconsiderations concerning the history of discrimination against Buraku and the use of discriminatory terms', in Buraku Liberation Research Institute (eds) *Long-suffering Brothers and Sisters, Unite!* Osaka: Buraku Kaihō Kenkyūjo, pp. 115–30.

Katō, Y. (2000) '"Seisabetsu" hyōgen hōdō ni motto hairyō o' ('More consideration needed in the reporting of sex discrimination expressions'), *Asahi Shimbun*, 15 February. Online at www.satsuben.or.jp/html/01lawyer/la11007.htm (accessed 30 September 2004).

Kawamoto, Y. (1995) *Sabetsu to Hyōgen: Kakuitsu KaraSai e (Discrimination and Language: From Uniformity to Difference)*. Tokyo: San'ichi Shobo.

Kim, M. (n.d.) *Aidenteitei e no Kyōhaku (Threats to Identity)*. Online at www.han.org/a/threat.html (accessed 9 December 2004).

Kobayashi, Y. (1995) *Declaration of Arrogance: Discriminatory Language Debated*. Tokyo: Gentōsha.

Koshida, K. (1993) 'From a "perishing people" to self-determination', *AMPO*, 24(3): 2–6.

Kotoba to Onna o kangaeru Kai (eds) (1985) *Kokugo Jiten no miru Josei Sabetsu (Discrimination against Women in Japanese Dictionaries)*. Tokyo: San'ichi Shobo.

Kusunoki, T. (2002) *Rights of Disabled Persons and Japan*. Online at www.hurights.or.jp/asia-pacific/no_29/04rightsdp.htm (accessed 16 December 2004).

Kyōdō Tsūshinsha (1999) *Kisha Handobukku (Journalists' Handbook)*, 8th edn. Tokyo: Kyodo News.

Lakoff, R. (1975) *Language and Women's Place*. New York: Harper & Row.

Landau, S. (1984) *Dictionaries: The Art and Craft of Lexicography*. New York: Scribner.

Leets, L. (2002) 'Experiencing hate speech: perceptions and responses to anti-Semitism and antigay speech', *Journal of Social Issues*, 58(2): 341–61.

McConnell-Ginet, S. (1998) 'The sexual (re)production of meaning: a discourse-based theory', in D. Cameron (ed.) *The Feminist Critique of Language: A Reader* (2nd edition). London: Routledge.

McGee, W.J. (1904) 'Strange races of men', *The World's Work*, 8. Online at www.boondocksnet.com/expos/wfe_1904_races.html (accessed 6 August 2002).

McLaughlin, J. (2000) 'Foreign worker groups protest Gov. Ishihara's racist remarks', *The New Observer*, May.

McNeill, D. (2001) *Media Intimidation in Japan: A Close Encounter with Hard Japanese Nationalism*. Online at www.japanesestudies.org.uk/discussionpapers/McNeill.html (accessed 3 December 2004).

Maher, J. (1995a) 'On being there: Korean in Japan', in J. Maher and K. Yashiro (eds) *Multilingual Japan*. Cleveland, OH: Multilingual Matters, pp. 87–101.

—— (1995b) 'The *Kakyo*: Chinese in Japan', in J. Maher and K. Yashiro (eds) *Multilingual Japan*. Cleveland, OH: Multilingual Matters, pp. 125–38.

*Mainichi Shimbun* (1999) 'Shina' to 'Chūgoku: a descriptive change in works of literature', 19 October. Online at www12.mainichi.co.jp/news/search-news/801356/8db795ca8cea-01.html (accessed 22 June 2000).

*Mainichi Shimbun* (2001a) 'Political correctness drives animal world crazy', 27 June. Online at http://mdn.mainichi.co.jp/news/archive/200106/27/20010627p2a00m0fp013001c.html (accessed 17 December 2004).

—— (2001b) 'Ainu blasts minister over racism', 3 July.

—— (2002) 'Survey reveals division in ruling camp on privacy bills', 11 May. Online at www12.mainichi.co.jp/news/mdn/searchnews/865992/human20rights20protection20bill-0-3.html (accessed 6 December 2002).

Marks, D. (1999) *Disability: Controversial Debates and Psychosocial Perspectives*. London: Routledge.

Matsuoka, T. (2004) 'Calling for the early enactment of a law on remedies for human rights violations', *Buraku Liberation News*, 131. Online at www.blhrri.org/blhrri_e/news/new131/new131-04.htm (accessed 25 November 2004).

Mayes, A. (2004) 'West has its way on "wogs"', *The Australian*, 21 October.

Ministry of Justice (2002) *The Law of Promotion of Measures for Human Rights Protection*. Online at www.moj.go.jp/ENGLISH/CLB/clb-05.html (accessed 6 December 2004).

Ministry of Justice (2003) *Heisei 14nenmatsu Genzai ni okeru Gaikokujintōrokusha Tōkei ni tsuite* (*Statistics on Foreign Residents of Japan as of the End of 2002*). Online at www.moj.go.jp/PRESS/030530-1/030530-1.html (accessed 20 February 2004).

Morioka, H. (1990) *Rakugo, The Popular Narrative Art of Japan*. Cambridge, MA: Council on East Asian Studies, Harvard University.

Morris-Suzuki, T. (1996) 'PC: a scapegoat gone feral', *The Australian*, 10 April.

—— (1998) *Re-inventing Japan: Time, Space, Nation*. Armonk, NY: M.E. Sharpe.

—— (2001) 'Packaging prejudice for the global marketplace: chauvinism incited by Tokyo Governor Ishihara', *Japan in the World*, 2 May. Online at www.iwanami.co.jp/jpworld/text/packaging01.html (accessed 9 December 2004).

Mushakoji, K. (2002) 'Go-aisatsu' ('A word of welcome'), *Furatto ni tsuite* (About Furatto). Online at www.jinken.ne.jp/about/index.html (accessed 11 December 2002).

Nagai, A. (1998) *Manga no Naka no Shōgaisha-tachi* (*Images of People with Disabilities in Comics*). Osaka: Kaihō Shuppan.

Nakamura, M. (1990) 'Women's sexuality in Japanese female terms', in N. McGloin (ed.) *Aspects of Japanese Women's Language*. Tokyo: Kuroshio Shuppan, pp. 147–63.

—— (1999) '"Kotoba" to chikara' ('Language and power') in S. Ide (ed.) *Kotoba ni miru josei : chotto matte, sono 'kotoba'*. Tokyo: Tokyo Josei Zaidan, pp. 41–68.

Namase K. (1994) *Shōgaisha to Sabetsugo* (*People with Disabilities and Discriminatory Language*). Tokyo: Akashi Shoten.

Narramore, T. (1997) 'The politics of rights and identity in Japan', *Pacific Review*, 10(1): 39–56.

National Association of Commercial Broadcasters in Japan (1999) *Broadcasting Standards*. Online (English version) at www.nab.or.jp/htm/english/nabstd99.PDF and (Japanese version) at www.nab.or.jp/htm/ethics/base.html#8? (accessed 30 September 2004).

Neary, I. (1989) *Political Protest and Social control in Pre-war Japan: The Origins of Buraku Liberation*. Manchester: Manchester University Press.

Nihon PEN Kurabu (ed.) (1995) *Sabetsu Hyōgen o kangaeru* (On Discriminatory Language). Tokyo: Kobunsha.

Nikkei (2003a) *Comparison between Japan and Overseas Media*. Online at www.nikkei.co.jp/ad/info/jpmarket/comparison.html (accessed 30 September 2004).

—— (2003b) *Newspapers in Japan*. Online at www.nikkei.co.jp/ad/info/jpmarket/paperinjp.html (accessed 30 September 2004).

No author given (1993) 'Chronology of contact: the Ainu and the Japanese', *AMPO*, 24(3): 26–9.

—— (1995) *J.I. Lee's Case*. Online at www.han.org/a/identity/adm2_lee_impeach.html (accessed 9 December 2004).

—— (1997) *A–Z Japan Collage*. Online at http://ourworld.compuserve.com/homepages/HFeid/home_2a.htm (accessed 7 August 2002).

Nohara, M. (1982) 'Kokusai shōgaishanen to masukomi no yakuwari: 21 seiki o mezasu "kotoba" no mondai' ('The International Year of Disabled Persons and the Role of the Media: the Problem of Language for the 21st Century'), *Rihabiriteishon Kenkyū*, 39: 40–3.

Nomura, G. (1993) 'Inauguration speech, U.N. General Assembly, 10 December 1992', *AMPO*, 24(3): 33–4.

O'Reilly, J. (1983) 'Women: a separate sphere', *Time*, 1 August: 69.

Oe, K. (1994) 'Hito o hagemasu bungaku no sōzō o' ('Creating literature which inspires people'), *Asahi Shimbun*, 10 May: 13.

Office of Government Information and Advertising (1997) *A Guide to the Use of Non-Discriminatory Language and Images in Government Information and Advertising Materials*. Online at www.ogia.gov.au/nondisgv.htm (accessed 11 May 2000).

Office of the High Commissioner for Human Rights (1969) *International Convention on the Elimination of All Forms of Racial Discrimination*.

REFERENCES

Online at www.unhchr.ch/html/menu3/b/d_icerd.htm (accessed 18 December 2004).

Okamoto, S. (1995) ' "Tasteless" Japanese: less "feminine" speech among young Japanese women', in K. Hall and M. Bucholtz (eds) *Gender Articulated: Language and the Socially Constructed Self*. London: Routledge, pp. 297–325.

Okano, K. and Tsuchiya, M. (1999) *Education in Contemporary Japan: Inequality and Diversity*. Cambridge: Cambridge University Press.

Ooms, H. (1996) *Tokugawa Village Practice: Class, Status, Power, Law*. Berkeley, CA: University of California Press.

Osaka Daigaku Buraku Kaihō Kenkyūkai (n.d.) http://dhva.phys.sci.osaka-u.ac.jp/~aoki/kaihouken/sabeturakugaki.html (accessed 19 November, 2002, site no longer live).

Oyama, M. (1994) *Kotoba to Sabetsu* (*Language and Discrimination*). Tokyo: Akashi Shoten.

Parker, G. (1999) *Limbless College Student Defies Japan's Notion of Disability*. Online at www.morningsun.net/stories/022900/usw_0229000017.shtml (accessed 14 December 2004).

Partridge, D. (2000) 'Outcry over mental illness movie', *Courier Mail*, 8 June.

Passin, H. (1955) 'Untouchability in the Far East', *Monumenta Nipponica*, 11(3): 247–67.

Pauwels, A. (1991) *Non-discriminatory Language*. Canberra: Australian Government Publishing Service.

*People's Daily* (2000) '*Ishihara's anti-China ravings castigated by overseas Chinese in Japan*'. Online at http://fpeng.peopledaily.com.cn/200004/14/eng20000414_38953.html (accessed 23 February 2004).

Queensland Public Sector Management Commission (1991) *No Offence: A Guide to Using Non-discriminatory Language*. Brisbane: Employment Equity Branch, Public Sector Management Commission.

Reber, E. (1999) '*Buraku mondai* in Japan: historical and modern perspectives and directions for the future', *Harvard Human Rights Journal*, 12: 297–359. Online at www.law.harvard.edu/studorgs/hrj/iss12/reber.shtml (accessed 5 December 2004).

Reynolds, K. (1999) 'Nihongo no Seisabetsu' ('Gender discrimination in Japanese'), in S. Ide (ed.) '*Kotoba' ni miru Josei*. Tokyo: Tokyo Josei Zaidan, pp. 213–52.

Romaine, S. (1999) *Communicating Gender*, Mahwah, NJ: Laurence Erlbaum Associates.

Roscoe, B. (1986) 'No place for the Ainu', *Far Eastern Economic Review*, 13: 66–7.

Ross, S. (1981) 'How words hurt: attitude, metaphor, and oppression', in M. Vetterling-Braggin (ed.) *Sexist Language: A Modern Philosophical Analysis*. Totowa, NJ: Littlefield, Adams, pp. 194–216.

Ryang, S. (1997) 'Categories and subjectivities in identification of North Koreans in Japan', *Journal of Asian and African Studies*, 32: 245–64.

—— (2002) 'Dead-end in a Korean ghetto: reading a complex identity in Gen Getsu's Akutagawa-winning novel *Where the Shadows Reside*', *Japanese Studies*, 22(1): 5–18.

Saitō, M. (1997) *Nihon no Shimbun, Seisabetsu Hyōgen ni Hajime no Gaidorainu* (First Guidelines on Gender-Discriminatory Expressions in Japanese Newspapers). Online at http://homepage.mac.com/saitohmasami/public_html/guideline.html (accessed 11 December 2004).

Sala, G. (1975) 'Protest and the Ainu of Hokkaido', *The Japan Interpreter*, 10(1): 44–65.

Savage Landor, A.H. (1893) *Alone with the Hairy Ainu, or, 3,800 Miles on a Pack Saddle in Yezo and a Cruise to the Kurile Islands*. London: J. Murray.

Schodt, F. (1983) *Manga! Manga! The World of Japanese Comics*. Tokyo: Kodansha International.

Sedler, R. (1992) 'The unconstitutionality of campus bans on "racist speech": the view from without and within', *University of Pittsburgh Law Review*, 53: 631–83.

Sexton, J. and Leys, N. (2004) 'Apology order for gay gibes on radio', *The Australian*, 23 November: 3.

Sherman, S. (1994) 'East meets West in the newsroom', *Columbia Journalism Review*, March–April. Online at www.cjr.org/archives.asp?url=/94/2/nhk.asp (accessed 5 December 2004).

Shikata, Y. (1998) *Masumedia ga tsukuru Jendaa* (*Media Constructions of Gender*). Online at www2.aik.co.jp/c-pro/shinfujin.josei/9812.html (accessed 24 January, 2000, site no longer live).

Shiomi, S. (1994) *Sakka to Sabetsugo* (*Writers and Discriminatory Language*). Tokyo: Akashi Shoten.

Shiomi, S. and Komatsu, Y. (1996) *Q & A 16: Dō koeru no ka? Buraku Mondai* (*How Can we Move Beyond Buraku Issues?*), Tokyo: Ryokufū Shuppan.

*Shōgai Fukushi* (undated) Online at www.ad-asahi.com/ikikata/ (accessed 14 December 2004).

Shute, S. (1981) 'Sexist language and sexism', in M. Vetterling-Braggin (ed.) *Sexist Language: A Modern Philosophical Analysis*. Totowa, NJ: Littlefield, Adams, pp. 23–33.

Siddle, R. (1993) 'Academic exploitation and indigenous resistance: the case of the Ainu', in N. Loos and T. Osanai (eds) *Indigenous Minorities and Education*. Tokyo: Sanyusha, pp. 40–51.

—— (1996) *Race, Resistance and the Ainu of Japan*. London: Routledge.

Siddle, R. (1997) 'Ainu: Japan's indigenous people', in M. Weiner (ed.) *Japan's Minorities: The Illusion of Homogeneity*. London: Routledge, pp. 17–49.

—— (2002) 'An epoch-making event? The 1997 Ainu Cultural Promotion Act and its impact', *Japan Forum*, 14(3): 405–23.

Sono, A. (1993) 'Freedom of speech in peril', *Japan Times*, 10 October.

Stevens, G. (2001) 'The Ainu and human rights', *Japanese Studies*, 21(2): 181–98.

Sugimoto, Y. (2003) *An Introduction to Japanese Society*. Cambridge: Cambridge University Press.

Sukigara, R. (1995) *Language and Discrimination: a Critical Examination of 'Sabetsu-go' in the Media*, unpublished Master of Arts thesis, International Christian University Japan, Tokyo.

Swain, J. and Cameron, C. (1999) 'Unless otherwise stated: discourses of labelling and identity in coming out', in M. Corker and S. French (eds) *Disability Discourse*. Buckingham: Open University Press, pp. 68–78.

Tabata, S. (2000) *Executive Summary: Discrimination and Hate in Cyberspace Observed in 2000*. Online at http://homepage2.nifty.com/jinkenken/eng3.htm (accessed 17 December 2004).

Tabata, S. (2001) 'Discriminatory messages are increasing on the Internet', *Buraku Liberation News*, 118: 6–8.

Taira, K. (1996) 'The Ainu in Japan', *International Education e-j*, 1(1). Online at www.canberra.edu.au/education/crie/1996-1997/ieej1/Ainu_ieej1.html (accessed 18 December 2004).

Tajima, Y., Uzaki, M. and Hattori, T. (1998) *Gendai Media to Hō (Today's Media and the Law)*. Tokyo: Sanseido.

Takagi, M. (1999) *Sabetsu Yōgo no Kiso Chishiki '99 (Basic Information on Discriminatory Language '99)*. Tokyo: Doyō Bijitsusha.

Tamiya, T. (1995) 'Sabetsugo to sabetsu hyōgen o kangaeru: gakusei no ankeeto chōsa ni motozuite' ('Thoughts on discriminatory language and discriminatory expressions, based on a survey of students'), *Kansai Daigaku Jinken Mondai Kenkyūshitsu Kiyō*, 31: 1–138.

Tanaka, H. (1991) *Zainichi Gaikokujin (Foreigners Resident in Japan)*. Tokyo: Iwanami Shoten.

Tanaka, S. (1993) *Japan's Orient: Rendering Pasts into History*. Berkeley, CA: University of California Press.

Taylor, V. (1997) 'Breaking literary taboos in Japan', *The Asia-Pacific Magazine*, 6/7: 39–40.

Thomson, R. (1997) *Extraordinary Bodies: Figuring Physical Disability in American Culture and Literature*. New York: Columbia University Press.

Tomonaga, K. (1997) 'The government-sponsored council for promoting human rights protection and the alternative council', *Buraku Liberation News*, 97. Online at http://blhrri.org/blhrri_e/news/new097/new09702.htm (accessed 16 December 2004).

—— (1998) 'A critique based on the present state of discrimination against Buraku people', *Buraku Liberation News*, 105. Online at http://blhrri.org/blhrri_e/news/new105/new10504.htm (accessed 13 December 2004).

—— (2001) *An NGO Briefing: Eliminating Caste Discrimination Around the World*. Online at http://blhrri.org/blhrri_e/news/new120/new12002.html (accessed 12 December 2004).

—— (2002a) 'Keynote address at the national assembly calling for the comprehensive revision of the Human Rights Protection Bill', *Buraku Liberation News*, 123. Online at www.blhrri.org/blhrri_e/news/new123/new123-1.htm (accessed 16 December 2004).

—— (2002b) 'Zainichi Kankoku, Chōsenjin e Bōkō, Kyōhaku ni taisuru Dankotaru Taiō o' ('A firm response to threats and assaults on Koreans living in Japan'), *Kenkyūjo Tsūshin*, 290. Online at www.blhrri.org/topics/topics_0039.html (accessed 12 December 2004).

Totsuka, M. (1993) 'The golf war on Mt. Kotan', *AMPO*, 24(3): 12–14.

Ueda, K. (1894) 'Kokugo to Kokka to' ('Our language and our nation'), in *Meiji Bunka Zenshū*, 44, Tokyo: Chikuma Shobō, pp. 108–13.

Ueno, C. (1987) 'The position of Japanese women reconsidered', *Current Anthropology*, 28(4): S75–84.

—— (1998) *Kitto Kangaerareru Seisabetsugo: Watashitachi no Gaidorainu (Sexist Language: Our Guidelines)*. Tokyo: Sanseido.

Uesugi, S. (1995) 'Buraku Kaihō Dōmei Dai 52Kai Zenkoku Taikai Hōkokushū' ('Report to the 52nd national meeting of the Buraku Liberation League'), *Buraku Kaihō*, 394: 13–94.

—— (1982) *World Programme of Action concerning Disabled Persons*. Online at www.un.org/esa/socdev/enable/diswpa00.htm (accessed 16 December 2004).

—— (2000) *The International Year of Disabled Persons 1981*. Online at www.un.org/esa/socdev/enable/disiydp.htm (accessed 28 June 2000).

UPIAS (1976) *Fundamental Principles of Disability*. London: Union of Physically Impaired Against Segregation.

US Department of State (2004) *Japan: Country Reports on Human Rights Practices 2003*. Online at www.state.gov/g/drl/rls/hrrpt/2003/27772.htm (accessed 25 November 2004).

—— (2000) *Country Reports on Human Rights Practices Japan 2000*. Online at www.state.gov/g/drl/rls/hrrpt/2000/eap/709.htm (accessed 9 December 2004).

Utsumi, A. *et al.* (1986) *Chōsenjin Sabetsu to Kotoba (Language and Anti-Korean Discrimination)*. Tokyo: Akashi Shoten.

Valentine, J. (1997) 'Skirting and suiting stereotypes: representations of marginalized sexualities in Japan', *Theory, Culture and Society*, 14(3): 57–85.

—— (1998) 'Naming the Other: power, politeness and the inflation of euphemisms', *Sociological Research Online*, 3(4). Online at www.socresonline.org.uk/3/4/7.html (accessed 9 December 2004).

—— (2001) 'Disabled discourse: hearing accounts of deafness constructed through Japanese television and film', *Disability & Society*, 16(5): 707–21.

Valentine, J. (2002) 'Naming and narrating disability in Japan', in M. Corke and T. Shakespeare (eds) *Disability/Postmodernity: Embodying Disability Theory*. London: Continuum, pp. 68–80.

Valian, V. (1981) 'Linguistics and feminism', in M. Vetterling-Braggin (ed.) *Sexist Language: A Modern Philosophical Analysis*. Totowa, NJ: Littlefield, Adams, pp. 68–80.

Van Dijk, T. (2000) 'New(s) racism: a discourse analytical approach', in S. Cottle (ed.) *Ethnic Minorities and the Media: Changing Cultural Boundaries*. Buckingham: Open University Press, pp. 33–59.

Walker, B. (1999) 'The early modern Japanese state and Ainu vaccinations: redefining the body politic 1799–1868', *Past and Present*, 163: 121–60.

Watanabe, T. (1995) *Kotowaza ni arawareta Seisabetsu (Gender Discrimination in Proverbs)*. Tokyo: Nanundo.

Wetherall, W. (1981) 'Public figures in popular culture: identity problems of minority heroes', in C. Lee and G. de Vos (eds) *Koreans in Japan Ethnic Conflict and Accommodation*. Berkeley, CA: University of California Press, pp. 281–303.

—— (1992a) 'Best not to mention: in Michael Crichton's *Rising Sun* a mention of the "unmentionable" became unmentionable', *Mainichi Daily News*, 8 November: 17. Online at http://members.jcom.home.ne.jp/yosha/minorities/waiwaicrichton.html (accessed 5 December 2004).

—— (1992b) 'The facts about buraku: recent media coverage', *Mainichi Daily News*, 1 November: 9. Online at http://members.jcom.home.ne.jp/yosha/minorities/waiwaiburaku.html (accessed 4 December 2004).

Wetherall, W. and de Vos, G. (1975) *Minorities in Japan*. Online at http://members.jcom.home.ne.jp/yosha/minorities/minoritiesjapan.html (accessed 9 December 2004).

Yagi, K. (1994) *Sabetsu Hyōgen no Shakaigaku (The Sociology of Discriminatory Expressions)*. Kyoto: Hōsei Shuppan.

Yamanaka, Ō. (1995) *'Sabetsu' to Media no Jiko Kisei ('Discrimination' and Media Self-regulation)*. Osaka: Buraku Mondai Kenkyūjo.

Yōgo to Sabetsu o kangaeru Shimpojiumu Jikkō Iinkai (eds) (1989) *Sabetsu Yōgo (Discriminatory Language)*, 3rd edn. Tokyo: Sekibunsha.

Yōrō, T. (1999) 'The fuss over brain death and the Japanese psyche', *Japan Echo*, 26(4). Online at www.japanecho.co.jp/sum/1999/b2604.html# (accessed 11 May 2000).

Yoshida, H. (1999) 'Fairy tales are falling victim to political correctness', *Views from Japan*, 4(4). Online at http://www.fpcj.jp/e/shiryo/vfj/99/4_4.html (accessed 17 December 2004).

Yuasa, T. (1994) *'Kotobagari' to Shuppan no Jiyū (Political Correctness and the Freedom to Publish)*. Tokyo: Akashi Shoten.

Yumoto, K. (1963) *Ainu no Kajin (Ainu Writers)*. Tokyo: Yoyosha.

Yunomae, T. (1995) 'Commodified sex: Japan's pornographic culture', *AMPO Japan-Asia Quarterly Review*, 25(4): 55–9.

Zenkokuren (n.d.) *Zenkokuren no Kyūdan Tōsō Sengen (Zenkokuren Declaration of Denunciation Struggle)*. Online at www.zenkokuren.org/internet.htm (accessed 26 August 2002).

# INDEX

CPSIA information can be obtained
at www.ICGtesting.com
Printed in the USA
LVHW011936080821
694812LV00019B/1329

9 780415 599337